AF422839

Shattered at Seven

Surviving Abuse, Addiction, and the Darkness That Nearly Took Me

Jessy Spruell

Preface to the 2026 Edition

When I first wrote this book, I was still learning how to face my past without letting it define me.

The memories in these pages were not easy to revisit. For years, they lived quietly in the background of my life—memories I carried but rarely spoke about. Like many people who grow up surrounded by addiction, chaos, and trauma, I learned early that silence could feel safer than truth.

But silence has a weight.

Eventually, I realized that the story I had spent so long trying to bury was the very thing that had shaped me. The pain, the confusion, the anger, and the shame were all part of the path that led me to the man I am today. Writing this book was never about reliving the darkness. It was about understanding it.

This story begins when I was five years old.

At that age, I didn't have the words to explain what was happening around me. I only knew the feeling of living in a world that could change without warning—where addiction, instability, and fear were woven into everyday life. As a child, I tried to make sense of things no child should have to understand.

For a long time, the scars from those years felt like proof that something inside me had been permanently broken.

I know now that they were something else.

They were reminders that I survived.

Since the first edition of this book, my life has continued to grow in ways I once believed were impossible. Healing did not arrive in one dramatic moment. It came slowly—through accountability, forgiveness, and the willingness to keep moving forward even when the past tried to pull me back.

One of the greatest blessings in my life today is my wife Shannon. She has shown me a kind of love that is steady, patient, and real. She didn't try to erase my past or pretend the scars weren't there. Instead, she stood beside me while I continued to grow and build a life that once felt completely out of reach.

Another part of my life that means more to me than I can fully describe is the relationship I now share with my father. Our story, like many families touched by addiction and hardship, was complicated for many years. But time, growth, and forgiveness allowed something new to grow where there was once pain.

Today, our relationship is strong. I respect him deeply, and I'm grateful for the bond we share now. It reminds me that healing doesn't only happen within a person—it can happen within families as well.

The events in this book remain exactly as I remember them. I have not softened them, because the truth deserves honesty. But I share this new edition with a deeper understanding than I had before:

Our beginnings do not have to determine our ending.

If you are reading this book and carrying the weight of your own past, I hope you take one simple truth from these pages:

What shattered you does not have to be the final chapter of your life.

Sometimes healing begins the moment we stop running from the past and choose instead to face it.

— **Jessy Spruell**

Contents

Prologue: Davis County Jail

If the officer had been two minutes later, my soul would have been in the abyss.

I stood behind a steel door with four small windows surrounded by cement walls, a toilet, and a small cement slab to lay on in case I was able to sleep. The cell was located in the infirmary in Davis County Jail, Utah. Gazing out the small windows, surrounded by the smell of sanitizers, I became transfixed by the scene before me.

I could see a woman. Though it was hard to make out her face, she had long black ratted hair, an inmate's uniform, and she was strapped to a hospital gurney.

She stared silently at the wall as a third nurse poked her with a needle, trying to find a vein. She winced and jerked. It should have been a simple blood draw, but after two and a half hours, attempt after attempt, they remained unsuccessful.

She had a certain unexplainable beauty. In another life, absent the torment inside, she might have been a beautiful angel. However, that would have been another life, and this was the reality, and in this realm of tangled shadow, her agony was forever present.

Her arms were covered with scars, mismarks, and veins bruised and blown by her most likely failed attempts to get high. To the officers and some of the nurses, she was just a junkie. I could see it in their uncaring faces, read it in their businesslike demeanor.

Thoughts flew through my mind. Had her uncle snuck into her room on countless nights, doing the unthinkable, stripping away her vital joy? Did she have an abusive mother who blamed her for her own failed relationships or beat her? Or had the hand of addiction sought her out for no reason other than by chance?

After multiple failed attempts to place an IV or simply do a blood draw, the woman was unable to get the medical care she needed, so the nurses returned her to her cell, and she instantly began to vomit.

I had tears running down my cheeks. I had so much to learn in life. So much love to accept into my soul, and all I could think was that I was exactly where I was supposed to be at that moment. I could witness this event because I was on suicide watch. I was on suicide watch because my pain—so similar to the pain that I could see in her face—took me to a dark place that I felt I could never get free from.

This is a story of my life. A tale of love, pain, and swimming the waters of addiction and agony.

I am beyond grateful to be here, beyond grateful to share what I have found, what I have experienced. How my own shadowy past wreaked havoc on my life. How addiction led me aimlessly through a fog, seeing but not truly seeing, experiencing life but not truly living.

My name is Jessy Spruell. I am writing this in a jail cell, reliving many experiences and trying to sift through them to find some light in this life, gain some understanding of how we create our own walls.

Eleven days before my thirtieth birthday, an officer found me in my cell with a sheet strapped around my neck.

I had created a dark temple of regrets. Brick by brick, it was constructed. Every thought was one of inescapable remorse, the gut-wrenching kind felt in the recesses of the core. I'd thrown away love, a life, and a business, only to find myself encircled by the dark temple of bricks once again.

It was not my time in incarceration that bothered me, it was the idea of possibly never having any solace, any inner joy, true love, or my own family. Such connectedness eluded me in this world.

This is how I got here. This is where my story begins.

Chapter One

River's Edge

My favorite thing to do as a child was to fish with my father, Michael Spruell. We walked down those beautiful rivers, the ones God dreamed of, and when he dreamed, they were created. The switchbacks cut the mountainside like a razor as the sun glistened off the crystal water. I didn't know where the river began and the sky ended.

I was five years old, and my heart yearned for the banks of Lower Fish Creek, Utah.

My father's effortless casts into the holes were an art form. His huge arms guided that tiny lure just where it needed to go. When he would catch one, he would let me reel it in and unhook it, depending on how bad it was snagged. Then up on his huge shoulders I would go and onto the next hole. This was my own heaven. It was perfect. He is my hero.

My brothers, Kenny and Jeremy, were with Mom by the truck when we came back from fishing. They were perched on a blanket, and I remember her huge smile as we approached. So beautiful; her brown eyes gazed upon us. It was one of those moments I sensed that she was actually present.

My parents had their own scars, and they buried the pain with addiction. My mother, Lori Spruell, was an angel in a wicked world. Her own type of angel. She strove to be here, but her emotional pain and thriving addiction constantly tried to take her over.

She lived fighting for joy and yearning for peace in her disjointed mind. I feel so bad now for how hard it was for her to live.

I remember shaking her on the couch when she was high, trying to wake her. It was as though Satan's arms were always pulling her under. She would stir, wake up, and gaze at me with those orange, jaundice-filled eyes. (The amount of pills she took caused the jaundice as her liver failed.) She loved her pills and her cigarettes. Between waking her and putting out the ashes she dropped on her blankets, my brothers and I would play Nintendo, eat ramen, and never stray too far away, lest she would not wake up.

In interludes between drug highs; when she was with us, she was kind and compassionate. She would be a mother. She would bathe us, cook for us, and chase us around with her dentures taken out. (Yeah, she had dentures at the age of twenty-nine.)

We lived in an apartment in the small town of Wellington, Utah. The apartment was one level with brown exterior trim and beige walls. The lawns were yellow because maintenance didn't water much. I always remember the lawn being too crisp under my feet to play on. This was a true disappointment. We wanted to play in the sprinklers as the summers were blistering hot, and we were bored out of our minds.

Kenny, my older brother, and I always kept an eye on Jeremy because he was the youngest. Jeremy and I looked alike at a young age, and I am two years younger than him. We both have brown eyes, light blond hair, and have perfect cue ball melons.

One of the neighborhood kids once decided to make fun of Jeremy, also affectionately called "JerBear" or "Bear." The teasing didn't sit right with me, and I punched the kid in the face a few times.

We were tight, my brothers and me, and everything in me pointed to "a loyalty that is cherished and never broken." Like a chain, our links were forged from the hardest steel. As long as we were one, we could survive all.

It was exhilarating to take my anger out on that neighborhood kid. As the bellows started, fire blazed inside me as my knuckles rapped against his skull. Kenny was playing nearby us when he saw the fight and pulled me off when I started seeing nothing but red.

You see, Kenny was the calm one. Older than me by two years and always thinking, calculating risk, cooking for us, cleaning us up, pretty much guiding us as a parent. Where he was the slow, methodical teacher, I was a make-it-or-break-it, risk-taking, bullheaded little brat. I was always seeking attention at any cost.

I was determined to break things, burn things, or cause any sort of destruction. My shadows (which I refer to as my dark side) were already growing.

At about that time, Dad got imprisoned. He'd allowed his own demons to grow, and his scars closed in around them, trapping him in his own cycle of pain.

My parents were swimming in their addiction to prescription medications; to escape their own realities, they wanted to be numb. I can only assume why they wanted to use drugs; I think at this point in their lives, it was to keep from going through withdrawals. So my father stole books of prescriptions from a doctor and started writing his own prescriptions.

When the law caught up to him, he had to take ownership for his actions. He was ripped out of our lives and sent to Utah State Prison.

Mom still had her ways to get high. We would come inside on those sunny days, close the door, and enter at night. We knew where she would be, stretched out on the couch, smoke rising from those hot cherries that slipped from her sleepy hands. So we did our duty trying to shake her into consciousness, making sure she was breathing or even had a pulse, and smothering out any potential fires from the cigarettes that would still be burning.

This phase of our existence didn't last long. I have an extremely difficult time now remembering how events transpired. I see brief moments in my mind as clear as a blue sky. Yet some moments are muddied or blurred together, time lines skewed or upside down.

My heart is true in this, my soul as one with these words on paper. Like a painting, I am trying to create my art, both seen and felt.

Addicts don't get high just for fun. We are dodging and running from a slithering past. The gates are open, and as we peek in, we creep farther into the tilted world of our own creation.

That's the double-edged sword of temporary reprieve from life's burdens. Our perception creates the level of torment. It's the memories that are carved into our makeup like stone. Our past does not define who we are; the experiences were founded by our choices. They shape us and build us, but that is it, only a layer in the ever-complicated visions behind us.

We allow ourselves to heal when we are ready. Ironically, the choice to run away from our problems only creates more pain. Pain that adds another scar.

Chapter Two

Prison Gates

I will always remember the confusion on my father's face when we first visited him in prison. My father's hazel watery eyes reflected this as my mother, brothers, and I walked into the visitors' room. He sat, arms on the table, staring at us. The drive had taken about three hours. I've never been a very patient individual, so I imagine I was a little brat in the car.

Utah State Prison is located at the "point of the mountain" in Draper, Utah. I will never forget the excitement I felt when we crested the point and saw the old ramshackle prison. As we entered, walking beneath the gun towers into the front gate, I felt the cold of the prison wrap me. The smell of correctional facilities was overwhelming. It's a combination of old wax from the floors, concrete, sanitizer, and the sour odor of human flesh that hasn't seen enough light. The total feel of the entrance was intense. The officers' black uniforms appeared menacing. These were my father's captors, and I vowed to hate anyone who came between my hero and me.

My father was in Lone Peak, a program awarded to inmates who avoided trouble. He fought forest fires and planted trees. He was in good shape from the work, and since he was in minimum security, I was allowed contact with him.

I ran into my father's arms, held by heaven. The sounds of the guard's radios were silenced, and we shook from anticipation. We cried together, all of us, our beautiful little family, striving for togetherness during our short-lived visit in the warm yard outside the prison.

They had a jungle gym for kids to play on. We boys consented to this bliss. It was as though we were a regular family at the park, if only I could forget that we would be stripped from the joy of our oneness. Seeing Mom and Dad happy, smiling, holding hands, gliding effortlessly in the sky of love. The sight felt so promising and complete. Yet I knew life was a roller coaster. A roller coaster with walls ahead, the tracks rusted, and the structure shaky, just waiting to fall apart at the slightest breeze.

My mom needed us to stay somewhere while she went to feed her addiction. We pulled up in front of Grandma Peggy's small blue rambler in Price, Utah. The old yellow Ford truck's brakes screeched loudly as we came to a stop. I looked over and saw that Grandma was out weeding her flower gardens.

Grandma Peggy is my father's mother. Grandma was married to my grandfather, Doyle Spruell, and they had three children together—father, Michael Spruell; Aunt Kelly, who is younger than my father; and Eddie Spruell, who is the oldest.

Grandma Peggy had a vibrant energy, a warm light that shone wherever she was as though her love embraced you without touch. Her round face smiled as we began to exit the truck.

She was Danish to the bones, big but not obese, tall but not a giant. She had a working woman's hands, callused from years of gardening and tinkering to stay busy. She didn't have a lazy bone in her body.

There were three apple trees in the front yard. A driveway separated two of them, and her tiny blue house is sitting slightly behind the two of the apple trees.

Every aspect of her yard exuded a certain frugal quality. Gravel in the driveway instead of concrete, a small cinder-block patio built with hand-me-down blocks, and an imperfect fence to the right of the yard. The wood underneath shone through the weathered white paint. Right by the fence lay a perfect flower garden where her tulips stood proud next to her daffodils, and the petunias helped the daffodils look even more at peace. This was her perfection, her pride and joy. Beauty came from not caring what others thought. She had a simple sanctuary, which she shared for herself and her loved ones.

Grandma's hands were covered in dirt as we approached. She was smiling ear to ear. Smiling so big you could see her soul shine through. So happy to see us, she sang a tune without words.

As we walked into her house, the heavy hardwood door opened and groaned as if pleading to be oiled. It sat crooked in its frame and dragged slightly on the brown carpet.

Grandma's house had two small bedrooms at the back and a living room connected to a kitchen in the front. Homemade rugs lay sporadic on the floors, and her mismatched secondhand furniture added to the warm environment.

I felt at war with myself, stoked to see Gram but torn apart because I knew we would not see Mom for a few weeks. This was the pattern; Mom could only handle us for so long, scudding across the tip of her relentless addiction. We were but pawns in a game. Her chemical romance seared her life.

I latched onto my mom's tight Levi jeans. Tears mixed with the smell of Marlboros. Normally, the smell of cigarettes on her was something I adored. That meant we were near to each other, where I knew she was safe. But the mingling of tears and smoke on this day caused an ocean of dread. My mind wandered, solitary in my own haunted ship, the waves annihilating my short-lived peace.

When she finally got me to release her leg, it was settled: she was leaving. I had to be strong, to admit to myself that nothing I could do would change her mind. So I wiped off my tears. I was sick of her seeing them. I had to man up, let her go. But when the door closed, I cried relentlessly on Grandma's shoulder. I hurt deeply as the old Ford pulled away.

I was home for now, where I could be me, minus the waves of addictions. Grateful to be with my brothers, inseparable. I looked into my grandma's eyes. They were rapture on a lonely shore.

Chapter Three

Sun-Drenched

We went to Creekview Elementary in Price, Utah. Grandma lived conveniently close by the school, only a few blocks away. We usually lived with Grandma during the school year. The school sat next to three domed structures that the city owned. They were used to hold salt for the roads in winter. They always piqued my curiosity.

My first grade teacher, Mrs. Tabiona, had the same type of 'fro as Grandma. She was strict but fair. Mostly, you could say she was just a good teacher who cared. She spoke softly, but when she got riled up, her tone would quickly silence us.

During that year, reading was my favorite subject. Mrs. Tabiona would sit on her stool and pour words into the air. Reading *My Side of the Mountain* and *Where the Red Fern Grows*, I held onto them, my imagination twirling, finding secret objects, and entering strange new lands never before seen.

I was scared of recess. My peers excluded me from activities, which was okay with me because I was never much of a follower.

But they said rude things to me about my clothes being ratty or my forehead too big. I took it all in, making it part of my identity. When

I looked into the mirror, my forehead seemed to go on forever or my clothes seemed to fall apart in front of me.

Every defect seemed to grow, and I withdrew further into my shell. I always ached for the day to end. I wanted to go home, to be away from everyone, to exist the way I wanted to in my own world where I meant something, where I was important like Indiana Jones or He-Man.

When the day ended, Ken and I bolted home to Grandma's. My amazing stash of Lego bricks and action figures were waiting to be torn into. Starships waited to be built, and action figures had to be put to the test in ultimate fights of valor.

Before Lego bricks though, I had a routine: upon arriving home, *Dr. Quinn, Medicine Woman* was always playing. I loved that series. We completed homework during the show. I sat there at the coffee table, diving into my lessons. After homework and *Dr. Quinn*, Grandma allowed us some Lego time, and then it was yard work. Oh my, I dreaded weeding out in the yard—the sun beating down on my back, sweating like crazy, stupid prickly weeds taking away from my toy time.

Grandma was strict. We had our routines, and she followed them to a T. Looking back, I realize how much I miss gardening and the by the book routines.

As wisdom grows and ignorance dissipates, I've learned that there is nothing in this life that resonates better with me than having my hands in the dirt. Planting gardens of any sort, tomatoes, peppers, bleeding hearts, or my grandma's favorite, petunias. Having the soft soil wrap my hands as I knead it like a handful of dough. Placing each plant where it feels right as the sun shines down; a gesture so tender, sparking life into the land of ruin. Alone in a paradise of temporary solace, I know I am creating something that transcends this physical plane.

I would always lie awake at Grandma's house at night, scared to be alone with my thoughts about Mom and her disease, about Dad and when he would be home. Falling asleep brought no escape. The dreams would come screaming from the base of my spine. Demons lurking, giant hands tearing me under the earth, and zombies with empty black eyes following me with death in their dead hearts.

I would wake up yelling, covered in cold sweat. Gram would already be by my side, assuring me that everything would be all right and covering my panic with a blanket of love. My angel she was, my other mother, and I cherished her more than I can ever describe with mere words.

Chapter Four

Shell of a Man

I missed my parents and lashed out by creating grand plans of deceit. Danny, my younger cousin by three months, and son to Kelly Spruell and Bobby Pike, was my partner in crime. He had been surrounded by similar living conditions as I and bestowed with the same character. When we were together, we created tornadoes, demolishing everything that stood in our way. If something was whole, we tore it into pieces. If it stood tall, we made it small, pummeling it into nothing. He was my other crazy half, and I feel terrible now for whoever had to babysit us in the wake of our wrath.

We would walk down the street to Guido's. The store was called Checkerboard Grocery, and Guido owned it. The store was located in Carbon Avenue in Price, Utah. The store was an old beatdown building that had been there for years. You probably wouldn't even have known it was a store if you were not a local. The Checkerboard Grocery sign had faded. Years of weather and sun had stripped it away. This did not matter because Guido catered to locals.

He had a wide array of the freshest fruit. Every melon you picked up had the sweet smell of ripeness, which took you away to the garden it had been grown in. The dairy was so fresh he might have owned the cows himself and processed the milk products with his gnarled hands.

Guido was Italian. He was rather short with a big nose and hair growing out of his ears. He always wore a white apron that looked like a medical shirt. His own style, something to remember him by.

There was never a day that he didn't smile. When we entered, he'd beam with delight, and always helped us with any selection. Superficiality didn't exist with Guido; he helped because he truly wanted to, not because of a false sense of customer service. You know, the need of wanting you back. You came back because it was Guido's.

The cash register was just inside the front door. On the counter, he had an old gumball machine that took pennies. Yes, pennies. That gives you some idea of when it was built. Guido always had pennies on the counter or gave us one so we could get a gumball. They were the best gumballs ever. It was a taste of Willie Wonka's every time I ate one with flavors bursting and scattering visions of chocolate rivers and gumball mountains.

Danny and I walked into the store one day with malice. Our plan was to steal some of those candy cigarettes with the little red tips. We thought they were so cool. Looking back, it tears my heart apart to think I could steal from the sweet old man. But at that time, my shadowed heart didn't see right or wrong. If I desired something, nothing would get in my way.

The idea of getting away with something nefarious seemed exciting. I wanted to prove I was that smooth. If I could pull it off, it would have been as if I had become invisible.

Thus I began to learn the art of stealing. Little did I know that this would rip me to smithereens, leaving me hollow and a shell of a man.

The plan was simple: Danny would create a distraction to pull Guido away from the register. We decided that Danny would "accidentally" drop his pocketknife behind the refrigerator unit so that Guido would have to go all the way around into the cooler to retrieve it. While he was in the cooler, I would slip behind the counter to where the candy was located.

Ironically, the candy cigarettes were by the real ones. I took two or three packs. I did not want to steal more than that; I wanted to avoid any attention.

We hung out for a minute to talk while guilt etched lashes on my back. The weight of what I had just done crushed me into the dirt. I could see God tallying giant marks on the wall, and I felt that Guido could see guilt written all over my face. My palms were sweaty, my hands shaking.

Once I got the door open, I couldn't get out of there fast enough. Like water through a crack, I bolted out. The wind struck my face, and I felt God staring at me. My blood froze with shame.

We cut down a small dirt alley between Guido's and a vacant building. Tumbleweeds veered toward us from a distant field, gaining momentum down the small alley. They looked like snowballs scooting down Mount Everest, getting bigger and bigger, faster and faster, a reminder of the deed we'd committed. We split left and right as dirt filled our eyes. God was mad, and he showed it.

So what did we do? We managed to get back to Gram's, to our hut at the back, and forget God's wrath as we opened the fake packs. We thought we were awesome as we puffed away.

Our hut was made of old pieces of plywood in varying sizes, leaning against bushes and brambles. They had been overgrown for years. At the center of the growth, where no one could see, was our favorite retreat. We had to crawl to get to it. Rocks kept up the plywood, and we had makeshift seats.

This was when I started stuffing my guilt away. Guilt for my theft, for my small lies, my swearing, and thinking about girls.

I doomed myself to a life in the world of fire where Satan sat with his horns, staring at me. He took my number along with those of all the other little thieves. Men with wings and weird trident tails flew above us. We were chained one by one, connected as Satan's new minions.

School carried on the same, the days passing in a dreary fog. They seemed a heavy procession, part of the clamor of the world. With my father's release, my hopes, wishes, and concerns would be fulfilled.

It was such a delightful day. The sun's rays shone brightly, cutting through the clouds' swelling breaks. The smell of bacon cooking overtook the senses as it popped and splattered in Grandma's huge cast-iron skillet. I was implanted in my seat, at one with the couch. With the window opened, I waited. My eyes were fixed on the curb as I expected my father's arrival at any minute.

Mom had left earlier that morning to go pick him up, and since then, I had been a ball of excitement. I didn't have to go to school, but I still put on my best clothes. I combed my hair just perfect, my normal hairdo, parted to the side with a dose of Rave holding my wave in place. Grandma loved the wave, the good ole Elvis look. As her huge hands shielded my eyes, she smothered my hair with the spray.

My patience barely held. My brothers were doing the same, trying to refrain from jumping out of their skin. In the distance, I heard the putter of the engine, distinct and nearing. My heart thumped; my stomach crawled. The butterflies inside flapped their wings to escape from their cocoons.

Then there they were, our parents, windows down and smoke filtering out. A flick as they shot the shared cigarette out. Their heads turned.

I was already to the door, and I froze. I felt shock. Was this real?

My dad seemed huge. His muscles shone. He had grown. He wore a white T-shirt, and his arms' veins surfaced like ripples in water. Rolled into his sleeve, on his shoulder, lay a pack of Marlboro Reds. He wore his hat with his long hair out the back, completing the image I remembered. My superhero better than Batman, Superman, and Spider-Man combined.

As we prepared to leave Grandma's house, I knew I was going to miss her, our nightly reading, and the old wall-heater warming us up in the morning. Her pancakes, miles thick and dry as a cotton ball so that gallons of syrup barely got them down. But more than anything, I would miss the way she smelled when she hugged me. The soft scent of light perfume combined with Dial soap—a blend so perfect that now when I close my eyes and sit back to relax, I can still feel her warm arms engulfing me, showing and saying without words, "Jessy, you're perfect. Jessy, I love you. Jessy, everything will be okay."

Chapter Five

On the Spot

We moved to Evanston, Wyoming, into a two-level complex, new and clean. It was a struggle to pack the furniture up those endless stairs. We helped with small things, but Dad did the most. He swore, lifted, and pushed. Damn, he was strong. Mom tried as best she could, but where she lacked, Dad picked up the slack.

Luckily, we did not have too much stuff. I am sure we lost a lot back in Price. We still had bunk beds, a couple of couches—one big and one small—a box TV with dials to change the channel, and never forget our regular Nintendo with Duck Hunter and Mario.

I loved Duck Hunt. I thought I was an expert at the ducks with six pixels squawking, and I shot them with my huge orange and gray gun, two feet away from the old box TV. How could one ever miss from that close? It was nuts.

I was perceptive at six years old. I saw the differences in love, the nature of different qualities in others, how certain things in people were adored more than others.

Dad loved us all in our own way. It was hard to understand the polarities, to understand that we were all different, because I saw us brothers all as being the same. We were brothers no matter what through thick and thin. We were one. Yeah, we fought and we argued, but if somebody hurt one of us, there would be no escaping the consequences from the others.

My mom had given birth to Ken prior to meeting my father. She had also name him the same name as his father. Kenneth Sr. was of Scottish descent and born into wealth. His family owned property on Nantucket, oil stock, and my brother was the last of the male bloodline to inherit that wealth. He was set to inherit it at the age of eighteen.

This caused huge waves in our family. Intentions were changed and manipulative ways tore through our family. The worst is that when families are torn apart, people fight about who gets what and when. This all happens when people are sick and dying. It blew me away.

Physically, Ken and I are very different. Ken has bright blue eyes, mine are brown. He is 5'7", I am 6'3". He has black hair, I sport dirty blond. Our mannerisms are the same; our chins are both round and prominent but not big.

We are close, and I will never forget the lengths he took to look after Bear and me. He is my little, big brother, and I love him dearly. There is nothing he could do that I wouldn't forgive.

I woke up each morning to Mom singing, the notes flowing. It was soothing.

It was my first day at a new school. I hated new schools, all the readjusting, trying to fit in, being poked and prodded. So I just listened to the tones of Mom's voice. I was home. It was solace.

Snoozing away in their beds were my brothers, dreaming of baseball fields and fishing reels, Tonka trucks, and flying. Dad was watching the news before work, and the smell of coffee suffused the house. The power of his presence was immense. My heart felt so grateful. It was complete. Nothing could get in my way; no one would bring me down. I would stand proud. We were one. Bullies didn't stand a chance; I would do what I wanted. Tetherball, monkey bars, it didn't matter. I was thinking this as I calmly drifted back to sleep.

I awoke to Mom kissing my cheek. I smiled and gave her a hug. The bed grasped me tightly. I wanted to stay in it forever; my flesh meshed into the waves of the cloth. The air surrounding me was like a mountain breeze, barely cool enough to need a sweater.

Dad was at work. We all rose to tackle the day. I felt sluggish. Parts of my warm bed still held on. I had to shake them off.

Sitting next to my bed was my brand-new pair of orange pump up, Reebok. And folded on my kicks was an outfit I'd picked out the night before. I can't tell you how good it felt to have a whole new outfit to wear.

Looking back, I actually remember the feeling I possessed prior to falling asleep. It was a peace I had never known. I had spent so much time being anxious and numb, waiting for all of the hard times to be behind us, countless hours wondering if we would ever be a normal family. The waves and pits in my stomach were finally gone. I dressed, splashed water on my face, and ate a bowl of Fruity Pebbles.

Wow, I was so naive.

Mom's eyes had the droopy look I had learned to fear. The poisons had once again claimed her. She slurred as she spoke.

How could she? Why? Here we were, finally one.

It was that quick, from soothing songs massaging my scars, warm kisses, and sweet hugs to the terror that came like a storm with darkness engulfing me. The sun's light was eclipsed by the pitch-black night.

I went to school in a horrible mood. It was my first day of first grade, and I had a fierce anger growing inside me.

I stomped into class a little late of course. Mom's Lortabs always threw off her sense of time. She could hardly hold her head up, let alone get us to school on time.

The school year had already started and that added to my visceral tremors. Cliques had already formed, alliances were set in stone, and coming to crash the party was the new kid from Price, Utah, the despicable outsider.

Ms. Nielson caught my eyes as I timidly entered. She had red hair that hung down to her shoulders. She was tall, thin, and her eyes were as blue as the morning sky. She almost eased my fear, but since everyone was already sitting at their desks, I could only feel their beady little eyes staring at me, sizing me up, and making quick judgments. I could literally hear the snickers, feel the kids pointing and joking.

Ms. Nielson must not have known I was so uncomfortable, but I knew she was going to make me introduce myself. I stood on the center stage and felt a slight tremor in my legs. Sweat started at the back of my knees. So I stood, took a deep breath of the warm, moist air, and tried to push out my name. It came out in a quavering knot of messy sound.

I felt like shrinking away. I wanted to hit rewind, go back, and try it all over. The laughter rose up, pushing me deeper into my emotional cave. I could feel the heat in my face. The heat seemed to melt me into the carpet where I stood.

My seat seemed to scream my name. I wanted to run to it, but I couldn't. I tried to be as casual as possible; I ran past the kids and heard snickering. My teacher's voice sounded sharp, like shards of glass, as she shut them all up.

At home, the brown pill bottles lay empty on the coffee table. Our family pictures hung crooked. In the pictures, we were all so happy. The poses seemed so effortless, the smiles so innocent and genuine.

Mom's addiction was as easy to read as a kid's storybook; it was written on her face. For Dad's, on the other hand, I had to feel and gauge based on the energy he presented. She had a certain sag to her face; she'd ingested so many narcotics. Dad didn't use as much; he tried to be more functionable.

If I wasn't looking, I wouldn't have noticed the switch. The pressure he held inside would explode, and he'd turn from the sweet, heartwarming hero that I adored to a menacing, uncontrollable puppet.

We were all puppets in addiction's hands. He pulled the strings one by one as he pushed the walls around us.

I stood there as my parents fought, and my strings stuck. I could do nothing but watch as Dad held Mom down. As he hit her, the echoes of her pain vibrated endlessly off the moving walls. The sound was empty as a black hole. Light went in never to return.

I was a coward. The trembling inside was torture.

Life wasn't always bad. There were blissful times as well. I ate those times up, every last crumb of the perfection, as if it were the last Butterfinger on earth.

Sometimes at night, we all sat around the TV on the couches, snuggling and watching *Flash*. I was usually in Dad's arms or by his feet. Ken and Bear were usually closer to Mom.

These were my first memories of Dad's legendary wink. Once I was coming out of the bathroom to sit back down and get back into *Flash*. I was in a hurry as I shut off the light. I looked at Dad as I bolted across the room, to avoid interrupting the show, and bam, he gave me the wink. His amazing, prideful smile. God, that wink was like a hug that lasted forever. It'll be like that for the rest of my life. The wink became part of our pact, our ritual.

As a kid, it is hard to see how patterns start; we don't act consciously, and the consequences follow us forever. We become a product of our environment. It is extremely difficult to break the patterns as an adult.

I was on the landing of our apartment, looking ahead, staring at the street. Beyond it, some small bike jumps rose in a field of weeds. Down a hill slightly farther than that stood another set of apartments. They were set up the same as ours, two levels with four apartments, side by side and front to front. It was early, the sun was just making its light known, the shadows were shrinking, birds sang effortlessly, and the last bits of green in the trees were bleeding to orange.

Mom and Dad were sleeping, and Ken was getting dressed so we could go play. Bear sat on the floor watching *Gummy Bears* on TV. The door was still open when the toaster popped. Bear whined about the chill I was letting in. So I shut the door and slathered a heap of butter all over my toast. I poured a small glass of milk and got Bear a bowl of Fruity Pebbles. We were trying to be as quiet as possible to allow our parents to sleep. Bear stayed home when Ken left for school one autumn day. I had a pocketknife and some matches on me, and I put on a sweater. Ken walked several paces ahead of me on the sidewalk. We headed to the field where Ken would kind of do his own thing, and I would make neat little forts.

It was one of those mornings when I felt at ease. Saturday and no school and the family home. There was still the constant reminder of the unknown, but we tried to make the best of it.

I arrived at the street, looked both ways. The coast was clear, and I scooted across.

Tall weeds skimmed my clothing as I entered the field. Moisture slid from the weeds to me. My hands had a little bit of chill, and the crisp air folded in around them. I heard Kenny with weeds crunching and rocks clinking beneath his feet. He'd brought some toys with him. I had mine too.

I started by cutting and ripping some weeds to create a small trail; my own trail led to an area where I could construct a hut. So I could sit.

I didn't mind being alone when I did this. Ken, I knew, was close, so it gave me a sense of comfort.

Also, I was trying to be sneaky. My little minion mind was reeling, the matches in my pocket calling to me. As I sat there on my butt, I took them out and they glowed. I held them in my hand, and the 7/11 marking glared back.

The sun shimmered far above, the dew-coated weeds were drying, and I had a grand idea. I decided to strike one of the matches and use it to light the whole book. Then I threw them into the tall weeds.

Ken saw the fire leave my hands and hightailed it out of there.

The fire took full rein. It seemed inclined to consume everything around it; it fanned and billowed about, scorching everything in its path.

I stood on the edge of an ocean of fire. Smoke rose, and I found myself intrigued by its power.

I was intrigued only until I realized I was going to get my butt whooped. Laced with fear and adrenaline, I fled home. Mom and Dad were still sleeping. I ran into my bedroom, shut my door, and twisted the lock, trembling.

After the local firemen came and smothered the fire, they banged on our door. Each time their knuckles connected, it felt like a jolt through my body.

I stayed locked in my bedroom. They stayed outside my door—my parents, the fire chief, and the police. I was a slave to the unknown. I was bound to be condemned to years of incarceration, or so I thought. My young mind churned.

I was actually left to my father's law although I received a stern talking-to from the authorities. My dad's law was a swift butt kicking.

I reminisce on that time, wondering why I started the field on fire. I don't think it was my intent, but when the opportunity arose, it seemed I had to create some peril, some act of destruction.

From that day on, at the age of six, my fears of consequences started to dissolve.

I was persuaded by false courage to just act, regardless of the outcome. A butt whooping only lasted a second and then the pain subsided. I learned how to disassociate from the physical pain. I don't know how, but it just didn't hurt, and I used this tactic of putting my mind somewhere else a lot throughout my life.

Chapter Six

On Ice

The roads were wet, slushy, and icy, a terrible combination to drive in. The road conditions spooked me, but my excitement for fishing far surpassed my fears.

We were headed to Fontenelle Reservoir in the barren Rocky Mountains. The winter was particularly harsh. I remember the snow being very deep and treacherous to walk through. My brothers sat in the back seat, and I was riding shotgun.

Dad had the window cracked for smoking, the heater struggled to work, and the fishing poles were stored in the trunk. Yeah, we were driving to the lake.

Luckily, Dad was an excellent driver. My trust in his driving ability has never lessened. Hell, he seemed better than any NASCAR driver.

I felt satisfied in knowing that we could escape from reality while spending quality time together, doing what I had determined to be the ultimate pastime.

The snowflakes were falling slowly. It was beautiful. Through small breaks in the clouds, the sky could be seen.

Dropped off in the distance lay the lake. Something caught my eye, something I had never seen before. Vehicles were littered across the lake. I had never known that ice could support pickups and minivans on water. But this was Wyoming, and Wyoming winters were cold to the bone.

Lynyrd Skynyrd's "Sweet Home Alabama" was playing in the cab of the car as we circled the lake and found a spot off the road to park. All we had left to do was pack our supplies to where Dad thought would be the best place to make a hole in the ice. Anticipation was eating me alive as he opened the trunk. I had my hands full and started to crunch my way in the snow toward Dad, trying to step in his foot holes. I could only land one foot in his hole. My other foot had to stomp a hole of its own.

We finally found our spot on the ice and set up chairs. Dad pushed the snow away so we sat directly on ice. Now came the tricky part. More like crazy, I should say.

Dad had a pick and a long piece of steel with a pointed end. He began to tear into the ice, beating, pounding, and sweating away. Three and a half feet in and three feet wide, he finally broke the thick Wyoming ice.

It was bitter cold. Winter's nip had my hands and nose tingling. When I finally got them warm, after my bait was set in the hole, it felt as if I had sat on my hands for hours. Tiny sensations, like little needles, tapped my skin.

Ken and Bear sat adjacent to me. Both of their noses were red. I looked at JerBear and noticed that he was starting to gain his own characteristics. His nose had started to grow into its own shape and size. His cheeks were round, mine were square.

I sat on my chair, pride fluttering inside. God, I loved this. Loved my brothers so damn much. It took everything I had not to get up and yell it at the top of my lungs.

Instead, I held my pole in my hand, watching Dad rig his up. He had so much confidence in his abilities when it came to fishing. The way that his huge hands spun knots, how he knew what bait to use to catch which fish and when. What Dad has is more than confidence. It is pure knowledge.

When we arrived home after hours of fishing, we found Mom asleep on the couch. I remember that the TV was on and blaring. The ashtray sat on the arm of the couch, packed plum full of butts. The air was too warm, but my heart felt cold when I saw her. I started to distance myself from her, started to pull away because I was sick of being let down.

This didn't affect Dad, though, because he held a huge four-pound rainbow trout, and we were headed to the sink to gut it.

Dad woke Mom to take a picture. She woke wobbly and sluggish. Her eyelids hung down as she crept toward us.

We boys held the rainbow trout, Ken on one end, me on the other, and JerBear sandwiched between. I will always remember this picture. I forced my smile. My anger flowed as Mom took it. Or attempted to.

Originally, Dad had his arms around us. But when the camera snapped, it was Dad behind it. Mom had been too high. I squeezed the fish so hard, my blood boiled, and just like that, my fake smile was captured on what had been, at one time, a perfect day.

Chapter Seven

Falling Away

Be warned, this was when a greater darkness started to veil our family more than ever before. I do have snatches of good memories. Honestly though, I feel and see only waves of shadows. I sit here at my desk in jail, trying to sort through what is in my memory. I see some smiles and fun but through a haze of pain. I truly try to see only times of light, but shrouding the light is a dark night.

Dad lost his job driving a truck, and I can tell you, I was glad when I heard that we got to go home to Price, Utah. I missed Grandma fiercely.

We were headed back home into the last stretch of the trip from Evanston, Wyoming, entering Spanish Fork Canyon. This stretch was one of many turns with mountains reaching into the sky and trees and creeks flittering by.

Helper, Utah, just kind of jumps out at you. The old coal town fits perfectly beside the electric coal plant. Plumes of smoke cover the sky and the book cliffs, which are mountains that resemble books sitting on their sides. This was Carbon County, my roots. It felt so good to be back. The empty sky above was a painting, orange fading to purple, purples to pink, and it all melted away from the blue. Not a cloud existed, just an open canvas where I could get lost by simply gazing into the space that was my escape.

We pulled into the town of Carbonville, Utah. Well, it was more like the street of Carbonville, and shortly after, we turned right onto A Street, which led to a hidden trailer park. That was where we would live. The first trailer you could see as you pull into the tiny offset park was ours.

The U-Haul came to a stop in the driveway. I heard Mom behind us roll to a stop as the gravel popped. The windows of the trailer had faded, yellow faux shutters. It was a single wide, and the skirting was busted up in places. It had a rotted wood staircase and small patio that led to the door.

Grass was virtually nonexistent, and behind the house lay a field with gray green Russian olive trees. The only good thing about these trees is the smell almost cloyingly sweet. They have massive thorns, more like spikes.

Our trailer home sat close to Price River. Cattails were scattered around, and the fishy and mossy smell of the river and the moisture of the fields scraped my nose. It presented the feel of marshland where we had endless activities to accommodate our empty time. It would be nice, I thought, to play in the expanse beyond, shoot BB guns and wrist-rockets, and of course, build hidden forts.

We had just gotten a brand-new lever-action BB gun, and the movie *A Christmas Story* rang in my head as I held it. The shiny black barrel, the amazing brown plastic wood-grain stock. A feeling of bravery climbed me every time I cocked a BB into the chamber. I considered myself one helluva shot.

Jeremy and I headed to a bunch of elm trees and bushes. I walked slowly so that Bear could keep up. Birds were flying and talking to each other, giving warning. The breeze was warm, and the smell of sagebrush filled my nose. We entered the canopy of the trees where nests rested comfortably in the branches. I planned on shooting a bird today. I wanted to see if I had the ability to hit something animated.

We trampled down a ravine. Halfway down, I went to my butt, feet out, and slid the rest of the way down using my feet for balance.

Bear struggled with this trick, so I caught him as he slipped. He called out for me, fear swelling in his eyes, and I pulled him closer to me.

Then I heard fluttering. My eyes flicked quick, and there it was: a tiny blue hummingbird, fifteen feet above me.

I lifted my gun and cocked it and took aim with my cheek resting on the stock; the bead of the sight honed in on it. My finger sweated on the trigger as I took a breath in and out. Just like that, I released the BB into the air.

I never thought in a million years I would strike it. It fell through the air, flapping its little wings as it hit the ground. My heart hurt so much as I approached it. It was doing circular motions all over, suffering. Its beak was blown off.

How could I have done such a thing? I wondered. What in the world had possessed me to be so evil, to kill such a beautiful bird? This creature was the spirit of beauty on earth. It had a living, beating heart, and only ever brought calm, serene smiles to people's faces. Here I was, a lost soul out wandering with dark intent, selfishly desiring a moving target!

It tore me to pieces. I knew then that I had to put it out of its misery. So I did it with another BB through its heart. Bear and I dug a small grave with a stick and our hands. We sat on the ground, the gun lying next to me. I put the hummingbird in the hole and slowly buried it, tears streaming down my little dark face.

I honestly didn't think that I would actually hit the heavenly life-form. But ever since I did, I began to look at myself differently. It felt as if the earth was cracking open and demons' clawed hands were reaching up to tear me to pieces, to kill me, and take me where I belonged. I didn't see it for what it was, a mistake that could be forgiven. I was my worst judge, striking myself down mightily, the gavel hitting me harder and harder.

We made it home as the sun began to fall behind the book cliffs. We had been gone for hours, and I am sure our parents were worried. Well, maybe. All I know is that I was extremely upset with myself about the soul I had taken away.

Bear went inside, but I wandered about. I wasn't done shooting for the day. The willows' leaves wisped as the breeze cut through them. I had my gun by my side, and my soul felt heavy. I was ready to shoot something, shoot anything, and there it was.

Right before me, shown by the dying sun's light, were those glass electric meter covers.

So, me being the little brat that I was, I started shooting them. I went from one to another to another. I made my rounds from trailer to trailer.

I'd almost shot all of them when I heard the neighbor yelling. In my foolishness, I ran home. The neighbor chased after me. He must have heard the glass shattering.

My legs pumped, gun flapping by my leg, and finally there it was ahead, our front steps. I ran from one end of the park to the other, gasping, fighting for air.

Dad was just coming out the door. The neighbor was cursing at me, veins in his neck ready to burst. But that ended instantly when Dad came off the porch.

The energy surrounding us seemed to implode. Dad's voice shook, and his body seemed to double in size. "No one will talk to my son like that," he said, and the neighbor bolted home faster than he'd been chasing me.

Dad wrapped the gun around his knee. The metal bent like hot butter, pieces of the gun shooting everywhere.

Next thing I felt was his size twelve shoe. The air bristled as it caught myself. I flew inside and zipped to my room.

I remember the little crazy smile I wore on the inside. I put on a show. I wanted to seem scared and sorry. In reality, I wasn't, but my punishment had ended.

Chapter Eight

New Insight

Once again, we attended Creekview Elementary in Price, Utah. I couldn't say that I was excited although I didn't feel a knot of anxiety as I usually did when entering a new school after the year had already begun.

The walk stretched on and on toward the bus stop. The dew ebbed on the edges of things; the warmth of the day had not yet begun. Just the breath of spring's morning. The trees with new leaves hung over the street, singing their tune as they rustled. The crispness of the breeze cut through my sweater as we pushed farther and farther.

We stood by the street, my hands in my pockets. Cars were fulfilling their daily routines, buzzing past us. Off in the distance I saw it, a flash of yellow as the bus made its way toward us.

The brakes hissed to a stop, and the doors opened inward, all in one motion. The bus driver had a bland smile plastered on his face as he waved us on. The clammy chill that had surrounded me evaporated when I entered the bus. My little legs took a huge stride as they stretched with each step. I will never forget the smell that drifted toward me, the smell of pungent BO mixed with old saliva as it drooled and dried out of their mouths.

My eyes wandered, and I saw that there were quite a few people in wheelchairs whose heads bowed to one side or the other. I noticed a glow about these people I had never seen before. So radiant, reflecting innocence and perfection. Their physical disabilities might have limited them, but inside their bodies were souls that weren't jaded by social darkness. They saw things through the glass of spirit, a gift bestowed upon them when others saw them as handicapped. To me, they revealed the wisdom of true happiness. This experience crafted a new way of seeing life and perceived limitations.

I made new friends on this bus, and I always held my head high as I exited with them when we arrived at school.

I knew some mean kids saw us differently. I saw them laugh among themselves with their little fingers pointing. At this time in my life, it did not affect me. I had grown and had started to see things differently. Yeah, I hurt and had my shadowy scars. But I was proud to have these disabled kids as my friends, and nothing would ever tear us down.

Chapter Nine

The Darkest Hours

My father's friend's house stood up a slight hill along winding, narrow streets in the small town of Kenilworth, Utah. The whole town had the underlying feeling of a ghost town where evil floated about freely and screams could be felt if not heard. We puttered up to the house, which had an odd angled awning and old wooden siding that was in shambles. A huge dead elm stood in the front yard.

I could imagine people hanging from the elm's crooked branches as we exited the car and approached the side door. My parents came because it was their friends' house, and they had a son whom we played with. Honestly though, every time we came to play, I had a feeling as if there were icicles above the door, but I had to cross under them to enter and hope that one won't fall and impale me.

My brothers and I got along okay with the son, Keith. Frankly though, I would much rather have just gone as far away as possible. The house had a musty smell of stale uncirculated air, combined with lazy attempts at cleanliness. You know, when someone just pushes around the nastiness instead of really cleaning. Overall, I just hated being there.

Our parents hung out, their addictions feeding off each other. In this phase of addiction, it was hard for them to see things for what they were. They had no real friends. They were merely selfish acquaintances, grabbing and holding according to Satan's will.

I remember we were playing hide-and-seek. There was one bedroom connected to a living room then a small flight of stairs up that led to two other bedrooms. My brothers and I were scattered everywhere as well as our friend. I participated, but my heart wasn't into it.

Honestly, hide-and-seek was always boring to me. My favorite thing to play was Lego. I got pretty good at building huge structures, and I imagined that one day I would live in one.

Anyway, Mom and Dad took off somewhere with my friend's mom, either to the store or to hook up on some dope, leaving us all under my friend's dad's watch.

He was in his room when I passed by. His eyes, black and hollow, slid over, and he called me into his room. It had a dresser with a mirror, all in one, and a large bed, one of those with the huge shelved headboards.

I felt like I had spiders crawling on my body as I entered. He asked if I wanted to watch TV with him, and before I could answer, the man who I saw as a demon stood up, swept toward the door, and shut it behind me.

It felt as if all the light in the universe vanished under a blanket of indescribable darkness. There was no escape. My heart began to pump more slowly, and I seemed to split into two, separating from myself. You would think that my heart would have sped up but not in this case. This was a room of pure evil, and I knew it.

He sat me on his bed. I was like a drone, mindless; my soul separated away. I don't want to recreate the heinous act he committed. Let me just say the shadows climbed the walls, pulling away all the light. My soul hid in a safe place as my body lay in night's rage!

I don't know how long his heinous act lasted. It felt like seconds, minutes, and hours shoved into days. He told me to never tell a soul, or he would kill my mom. But no one would believe me anyway.

When my soul found my body, part of it had been left somewhere.

The scars grew deeper inside me. I felt dirty and scared to tell anyone. I thought I was weak for not stopping it. Had I wanted it? What was wrong with me? I couldn't tell a soul. Not only did I want to protect my mom, but I didn't want Dad to see me as weak.

Thus began my darkest secret, one that I lived with until I was nineteen years old.

Every day, I thought about that evil man. The nightmares sent me into fits of shock. Ken held me at night. The sickness of that man haunted me. I carried another shadow now. It was dark, it was so damn dark, and nothing I could do would get it out of my head. It was a festering wound, spreading, and consuming all the light that remained in me.

The cycle of pain is only broken by choice and willpower. My pain, my shame, my weakness brought me to the brink of death on more than one occasion. I stood on the fence, seeing the flames beyond, and tried to fall into the abyss. God's arms reached and heavenly hands, who knew that there was so much more for me in life, held me.

I learned that I can teach others that there is a light wherever you look. The tornado of addiction can be stopped, and we can overcome all odds with love.

Chapter Ten

Bliss

I sat at the kitchen table at Grandma's house. She had me watch her do the dishes. She was set in her ways, and I would learn the proper sequence and method of hand dishwashing. She didn't believe in dishwashers. Not to mention there wasn't enough room in her kitchen to have one.

All of her cupboards were painted white. She had a total of ten, including wall and base cabinets. In the corner to the right stood her pantry, which held a variety of generic foods.

The old wall heater stood close to the pantry. My brothers and I had many fights about who got to sit in front of the old wall heater.

We had been spending more time at Gram's house after school doing homework. I caught some of *Dr. Quinn* and enjoyed the placid environment. Our parents happily allotted Gram this time, and I began to enjoy it.

Gram's alabaster skin had an essence that words completely fall short in describing. She rolled up her sleeves when she flipped burgers, and I noticed sunspots.

She had lupus. I never knew what that was, but I sensed that in conjunction with her diabetes, it wasn't good. I always wondered how it would be to have to poke yourself in the stomach with a needle twice a day. Gram was a trooper, and nothing slowed her down.

The day was fizzling, clouds fat and fluffy, and we were all grateful for the sun's brief departure. The intense summer heat was maddening, but family barbecues always brought miles of smiles to my face. Lots of laughs, Uncle Troy's persistent tickling, and all of us kids roaming Grandma's sanctuary. We were all together.

Uncle Troy, born to Troy Sr., was the love of Grandma Peggy's life. He unfortunately died of poisoning from Agent Orange after the Vietnam War. Grandma Peggy had been married to Grandpa Doyle for years. After the divorce, she drifted into Troy's loving arms.

It was at this time that I made my first memories of my sister, Allissa, who is six years older than me and the daughter of my dad and his first wife, Tracy. Allissa lived with her mom, so we only saw her every once in a while.

I have always looked up to her. She carries an air of confidence wherever she goes, captivating all those in her presence, but we hold each other close in our souls, and we read each other's emotions. The filament of energy we share is complex; I will never take this for granted.

We ran into each other's arms. She looked like Dad, not in a manly way but with a soft, elegant difference in facial structure. Dad has a square jawline and chin; Alissa's was a bit rounder. Her hair tumbled about, gracefully brown, and her smile was so sweet.

I felt giddy with excitement as we all ran around that year, being kids. It was Ken, Bear, Allissa, and our cousins Cody and Danny, and never forget the big, little kid, Uncle Troy.

We all felt the effects of the hands of addiction. Like a clothes wringer, it stripped us of so much innocence. It played a huge role in all of our lives. I can't go into too much detail about how it affected others because this is my story and it wouldn't be fair to them. I just know that on this beautiful barbecue day, we felt all seemed to feel weightless with joy, flying in our own temporary happiness and out of the wasteland of our lives.

It was late at night, past bedtime for sure, and Mom was lit on her pills. We were waiting for Dad to come home. We didn't know where he was, and we were growing worried.

We came to the living room when the phone began to ring. Mom sat in the recliner, sleeping. It rang and rang, louder and louder.

I already knew who it was before Ken picked up the receiver. It was a collect call, and I shook Mom awake to accept it. Lo and behold, it was Dad, in jail, calling to tell us he loved us.

Dad had still been on parole and had been picked up on suspicion of some other fraudulent charges.

The sickness I felt was like a punch in the gut, wind knocked out, so I had to fight with all that was in me for one more breath.

Tears couldn't flow, and once again, I separated my body from my soul. I took the pain from my father, breathed it in, held onto it, and twisted it into self-hate. If I hated myself for the pain my father caused, making it my fault, then I wouldn't feel toward him what I felt toward Mom.

So grew the cycle of my inner hate, enclosing in my scars the guilt I felt for allowing that man to molest me. My second shadow was the secrets and the flow of shame beating in my tainted heart.

The days grew longer, gloomier, and fell into more forlorn patterns. Mom fell into the darkest pit I had ever seen. I watched her shatter into pieces. The inner pain made her useless. The couch held her tight as her weakness edged to the surface.

We started to miss school more, sleeping in, and waking up to hours of Nintendo. Waking up, we ate the same old things: ramen noodles, cereal, and whatever else we boys could scrape up.

Chapter Eleven

Stripped Away

I remember the rain spattering on the roof of our trailer. It sounded like cannonballs, then it fell off the side, and the ground soaked up the rest. I was completely absorbed in to Mario, having just switched from Duck Hunt. I was just using the flute to skip lands and levels when I heard footsteps on the porch, followed by knocking on the door.

Ken opened the door. The people outside were a man and a woman. They had umbrellas and were dressed professionally. The woman held a clipboard of some sort. All I felt was baffled. Their aura was intimidating, and the clipboard seemed to reflect their intent.

My fears were amplified when they asked for Mom. *Oh crap!* She was lit in her room, and no matter what, these people would see the person that the drugs had taken over.

I felt resentment toward Mom. Still, I didn't want to be yanked away from her. We were her guardians, and I didn't know what to expect if we were to be separated.

As I stream further back in my mind, tunneling through the ups and downs, I see that I just hurt tremendously. I missed my *mom*, not the person the drugs had made. I missed her calm, beautiful smile, her soft voice tenderly waking me, and the way that she glowed brighter than the rays of the rising sun.

She was my mother for hell's sake. I wanted her back. I had put up the walls to protect myself, to drive away pain. But the mask I wore was as thin as paper. I longed for her love. I ached for it beyond comprehension. So on the day the Department of Child Protective Services took us away from her tired hands, I shattered inside. Both halves of me twirled down a tornado of fire. The shadows behind me laughed, holding on as I screamed and pleaded to be released to my mom.

My first memory after being stripped from Mom was the smell of dank horse manure. Wellington, Utah's wind blew the smell around aimlessly. There was no escape, and eventually, I just grew used to it.

Grandma couldn't take us until she was approved by Division of Family Services. Which took about a month. So we had to tough it out, be patient, and have faith that Gram would save us.

We stayed in the basement in a home literally houses down from our first apartment in Wellington, Utah. I met my foster parents, but I don't remember what they looked like. I can't paint a description. I must have pushed them out of my mind for one reason or another. They had two children, a boy about Ken's age and a girl about my age.

The beds we laid in were not ours, and I felt a well of unease. Each bucket from the well felt tepid. As I aspired to bring the water closer, I felt it was tainted by the unseen.

The blankets that covered me reeked of someone else's comfort. I was so used to my own smells, and the swamp I felt I was swimming in brought complete terror.

Sometimes, when it comes to foster homes, siblings are torn apart. This would have devastated us. God had his angels among us. Through the dark clouds, we flew as his angels held us.

We had oatmeal for breakfast and then off to the stables Ken and I went. We shoveled horse manure; it was part of the routine. Each shovelful got heavier and heavier. I hated the smell so much and the constant list of chores.

Then it was lunch. Can you guess what it was? Yeah, oatmeal.

Creeping around the corner came dinner, and we found another bowl of overcooked, mushy, unsweetened, nasty oatmeal sitting on the table.

This was a precarious time in our lives. The foster parents used to cook things like meat loaf and potatoes for their own children, and we ate bowls of oatmeal. I was so envious of their delight. My mouth watered as they ate, and the foster parents made us shove down our slop, spoonful by spoonful.

There's a part about the foster system that is illusionary. It's simply a roll of the dice. You never know what number you will get.

The gamble that was our lives kept rolling. The experience glazed one layer of hate on top of another. We seemed to be stomping with heavy feet on thin ice with a void below aching for our demise.

So between, I punched the neighbor in the face in Wellington the first time until our return as fosters was almost two years. Dad did eighteen months in prison the first time, we lived in Evanston, Wyoming, briefly, and then drifted to Carbonville.

The words I have used to share, my emotional ebbs and flows, I pull directly from the core of my soul. I want to heal, to douse the fire. I feel shifts in the flames burning inside as if they are slowly smoldering away. Every day, I get less angry, and at night, I pray for the ability to pull out of the flame enough to write. I have shed so many secrets, cried, and not held back.

It was lunchtime. My brothers and I were eating at the kitchen table. Our foster family had already eaten, so now it was our turn. The smell of their meal slowly meandering out the cracked windows.

I looked out the window as I slowly shoveled another spoonful of the goop into my mouth. The taste was repugnant as it meandered its way down my throat. I would be so glad when this time was over, when I could be home with my family.

I grew impatient. I felt no love from these people. They were merely slave-drivers. Each day we cleaned the barns. Wading through tons of horse dung that had grown beyond reproachful with the scummy flies buzzing by. My muscles ached. Hell, they were fried.

We looked at each other, my brothers and I. Our young minds spun and wondered why. Ken smiled, I remember, and put his hand on mine. Bear sat there, and I winked at him twice. God loved us dearly; I know this now. I knew it then, but hate shoved the knowledge of it down.

I glanced toward the sound of a car I heard approaching on the gravel driveway. I knew it before I saw it, but the white 'fro proved it. *Yay!*

Gram's car came to a stop, and I flew out of my seat. She was just as fast as she came to the door. I rejoiced in knowing that we were done. I saw it in her smile.

It's etched in my memory and always will be.

She had her big dollar-store sunglasses on, and her massive Danish hands went to knock. But before she could, I beat her to it. We were done! I felt like flying away.

My brothers and I cried as she held us. It felt as if she stood above our deep hole with a rope thrown down to rescue us, inch by inch. We were going home, aching and starving for something new.

Later, we all sat on Gram's back patio. She had saved us from the concentration camp we'd been in, and relief flooded through me as we ate our first delicious meal in a month.

Our clothes blew on the clothesline, and the distant horizon shone pink as the drowsy sun fell away. The grass looked beyond inviting. It had been a while since we had played, and my feet were ready to feel the tiny blades between my toes.

Grandma had jumped through all of the state's hoops to eventually get her own foster care license.

Her sacrifices were abundant, and her jovial laugh sent pulses of love through me. Her laugh came from her stomach, sincere on every level. She was an angel from heaven, pure in form and pure in soul.

The days trickled by, blending into each other. Times were good. We had our routines back. I started to appreciate weeding in the garden more or doing the dishes. Chores at Grandma's were nothing compared to the slave camp we'd been at.

We started to see Mom more. She would come by once a week, and she looked like herself again. Her soft smile, her eyes beautiful as could be, and the way she hugged us as if she never wanted to let go.

The only thing missing was Dad, and I thought of him constantly, always wondering when he would be out. I missed fishing with him, listening to the rivers splashing the rocks, and seeing the fish flopping through the air as the "artist" hooked one. I missed falling asleep on his chest, his huge arms wrapped around me, and his hissing snore pushing me to dreamland where I had kid dreams that weren't demonic.

Chapter Twelve

Leaving Behind

Mom released the Frisbee, and my little legs pumped as I bolted toward it. The Frisbee was warm and moist, my hands were covered with sweat, and I almost had hold of it when it slipped. Ken was a distance off to my right, and Bear Bear was excited, wanting to play too.

We were at the park in Price, Utah, and the massive trees reached high, almost blocking the sun's direct light. People laughed in the distance, and kids frolicked about, like us, their joy spinning the park's warm air. I felt at peace, seeing the light in Mom, feeling her calm and assuring love. She was truly herself once more, and I loved it. Her presence was healing. I almost forgot about the scars, about the pestilential wounds festering inside. But most of all, I forgot about my second shadow, the dark shame, the secret that I vowed to take to a deep grave. I embraced this moment, effortlessly enjoying the time being us.

It was official, the day was finally here. After x months, the long wait was over. My dad was getting out of prison. No more lying awake at night with my mind wandering, feelings churning, and anxiety boiling in my stomach.

This time, my brothers and I cruised up to the prison with Gram to pick Dad up. We passed rivers beside us, pine trees, and the beauty beyond waiting to be fished. It felt like Grandma was going as fast as a dying snail.

The sun was pushing pale purples away. I looked up, breathing Draper's air in through my nose. Seagulls were flying, and I remembered hang gliders flying off of the point of the mountain.

Dad was due to get out at 8:45 a.m. I leaned against the warm front of the car. The parking lot was fairly empty, and I was still struck on how amazing it was that men were flying in hang gliders above. I wondered how they did it, how they got the nerve. I knew they took wind off the point of the mountain and stepped into fake wings. Metal bars to hold on to, feet dangling about, and the ground waiting to taste blood at the brink of fast winds.

I leveled my eyes to the prison's exit, and I saw him. He beamed as he strode toward us, a bag in his hand. Once again, he looked bigger, muscles bulging in his plain white T-shirt.

I could see that the poisons in him had abated. I was stoked to know that his active addiction had been silenced. The ruin caused by drugs had been left behind.

His voice was broken as he spoke, and the tears in his eyes shone. The winter of ashes we had lived in was once again put behind us.

My parents wouldn't be together though. My brothers and I lived with Grandma, and Dad stayed in a camper outside until he could find us a place.

Mom would come and see us. Each time she did, I felt lighter and lighter. The calm energy surrounding her was like lying in a field of flowers, staring at the changing shapes of the clouds, and breathing in the sweet smell of forever.

First thing in the morning, as the sun began to rise, I grabbed the fishing poles and put them in the trunk of the car. My brothers grabbed the rest of the food, and Dad told Gram we were headed to Electric Lake, Utah.

Like every other time in my life, the anticipation of fishing ate me alive. I have a one-track mind, basically on autopilot, and the jolt it sends through my body when I reel a fish in is simply unexplainable.

The mountains stood boastfully. Aspens sheathed the expanse, and the summer's wind swept by as we drove faster toward our destination. As we came to the last stretch of our descent, the sunlight was reflecting off the blue beyond as the mountain's edge mirrored its perfection. Dad winked at me as we started to pull off a dirt road. My brothers, in the back seat, were as excited as me and ready to tear into the water. Fishing was in our blood, born and bred. Nothing would ever change that. Mom was safe, and that vast sanctuary brought us deserved ease.

We pulled off the side of the road, dirt filtering behind as the breeze took hold. We drove around the lake to where the rivers and creeks all met to become one, the inlet that feeds the giant man-made pond.

Dad kept true to his promise although it was nine months late. I remembered the pain, knowing we were going fishing the next day but getting that dreadful phone call from Dad saying that we weren't. But I fitted it somewhere inside, pushed it into some buried place.

I headed down the green marshy grass. I halted and brought my eyes to the image past the vitreous edge. The lake and aspens and pines stretched before me.

It was a canvas of God. He'd literally painted it himself. His love etched each tiny detail as if he spoke with each stroke of the brush. Crisp wrinkles in the water, blinking and humming to a hardened soul. This was heaven. This was bliss. Thank you, God, for this.

We continued walking toward the inlets. There were a number of small streams coming off the side of the mountain. I reached one of them and had to jump. Dad stepped over, holding Bear. Ken strode right beside me amid tons of tiny jittery gnats finding temporary refuge in the corners of our eyes and ears. I could walk for a distance and run into a few then soon I would hit a pesky swarm.

Eventually, we reached the bank where Dad decided to end the journey. He told us to go find sticks to hold up our poles. So we roamed, trying to spot our makeshift tripod.

While we were doing this, he set up rocks to sit on and also rigged up our poles. I stomped around, my legs pumping about. No one existed except us, four sets of smiles, the four boys of our family out being men.

The fish weren't biting, and the streams challenged us to fished. We grew impatient with where we were positioned on the lake. We reeled in our poles, and I looked at the cheese on my hook. There hadn't been even a nibble. The others reeled in theirs, with the same results, and we left most of our stuff to hit the streams.

We all followed Dad. His huge steps gained speed as his excitement grew. Dad has never been a lake fisherman; he was born for the rivers. After the time we'd spent fishing with no luck, weariness spurred desire, and he was now on a mission.

This was how it became in life for our pack. Lakes were boring to us, so we found passion in walking the rivers. It took practice to understand the river's flow, knowing where the lure should be thrown, visualizing where I would be if I were a fish, branches going over the water, banks providing amounts of shade.

With the flick of the wrist, my jig mimicked a dying fish. Eventually, it seemed to become part of the DNA, one with the pole, reels, and lure. I learned to feel the wind, gauging the speed and direction. All of this creates a purpose. Lake fishing can't hold a candle to this.

The heat picked up as the sun beamed directly above. The sky was baby blue and clear as glass, and a cloud didn't exist. I had sweat on the back of my neck as we sat to eat some lunch. It had been an amazing day full of catching fish and spending time with my dad and my brothers. We all had a tint of red beginning to form from lack of sunscreen.

Off in the distance, we saw a tail of dirt being led by a vehicle. It was driving toward us. Dad knew what it was before it grew near. It was a sheriff.

The sheriff got out of his truck and started to come our way. I grew nervous, thinking he was coming for Dad, but Dad seemed at ease. As he approached, he called Dad over. I stood watching the conversation and following their body language.

Next thing I knew, we were running to our car, leaving everything behind. Dad carried Bear. I didn't know what to think as we followed the sheriff. Dad didn't say a thing except that we needed to get to the nearest phone. I had a terrible feeling in my stomach, churning and turning like never before.

The road signs flew by, and when I looked at the dotted line on the road, it appeared solid.

Dad was focused on the road ahead. He took the twist and turns of the canyon as if he owned them. Transition from gas to brake to gas was perfect. The sheriff didn't care that we passed him. We were all silent as we pulled into the old mountain's convenience store. All I heard was the gravel as we skidded to a stop.

Dad left the windows rolled down when he went into the store. He moved so quickly it was as if he couldn't get in there fast enough. I opened the car door, still sitting in the front seat. Then I heard the sheriff pull in behind.

It seemed as if Dad had been in the store forever, and I was growing sick. I thought I would vomit. The mountains were starting to gain a certain vileness. We were far from home, and I knew something was wrong.

When Dad came out, he seemed to carry the weight of the world on his shoulders. He looked defeated; he had the face of a haunted man.

It felt as if invisible doors were closing in on me and swiftly locking. Lights were being shut off one by one, shadows engulfing me. I thought that God had pulled back the gray, the curtains of pain, but I was utterly incorrect. The screams of shattered hearts came from below.

Dad got down on one knee, tears streaming down his face, and told us. Mom was gone. She had died.

My soul separated.

My shadows were menacing, pulling on my soul. God, I felt heavy. God, I hated you.

I couldn't find a tear. My chest was caving in, and I sat there staring blankly ahead. Why had I tried to be happy? Darkness spread through me like oil on water, lingering effects of Satan's intense grasp. I was seven years old, and my blood was pumping black.

Every time I began to trust, to allow, I was folded backward. Sheets of pain convinced me I was trash, converting forward to elapse to black. Nights took over, days were shaded, and I was captured somewhere between my two shadows.

My mother's death was extremely difficult to comprehend. We had all been seeing her change, the love she spread, and the light in her soul. I couldn't see her death for what it was, an accident. Drugs' illusions will leave a person dormant. I didn't know that her pain was slowly swallowing her, that the shadows of her past still haunted her.

I had been truly moving forward, trying to trust more, and tearing down walls brick by brick. All I knew now was hate. It was easier to hate than to hurt. Webs of deceit, webs of longing crushed me.

My fears started to grow. I never wanted to get close to anyone again. I became a zombie. Shades of darkness veiled me. God, I just wanted love, why did you do this to me? Rest in peace, Mom, in your shallow grave.

I was so mad. Why me? Why us? Were we burdens? Weren't we worthy to see the light and stay away from the poisons?

I breathed in shallow wisps of gray. Light was blocked as I cried inside. God, this is your fault! So I never opened up. Swallowed by fear, fear became me.

I understand now, I truly do. I see the truth for what it is. God won't dole out what I can't handle. There is a purpose in all limits he tests us with.

Words written between the lines have helped so much. I have never tried to forgive her, but since I began my story, light has pierced more, and my perception of forgiveness has changed.

My own addiction has helped me to see the struggle that comes when we are not able to leave out the poisons. What's ironic is that the very drug that killed her brought me here. I never thought I would love the brown pill bottles.

The funeral was masked by a sunless day. Indistinct conversations were muttered around me as I sat in my chair. Gloomy music was played, and the iciness of the room created goose bumps on my flesh. I was engaged in my own thoughts, distant and empty. I felt abandoned by love and incapacitated. I still didn't cry. I was a sponge that couldn't be squeezed.

Her casket was white, sitting at the front of the room. It seemed miles away, and I was scared to go near it. That was where her shell lay. I understood death. I knew that now her biological machine was destroyed.

My eyes were burning and dry as medicated cotton. Dad sat by my side, trying to hide his pain, to stay strong for my brothers and me.

I looked over at Grandma and Grandpa Davis. They were overwhelmed with sadness, tears streaming down their faces. Next to them sat their two remaining children, Aunt Michele and Aunt Cyndi, who had lost their dear sister.

We were all afflicted by God's hand. There had to be a reason for this sting, for this burn. The torment twisted, aching and ulcerated.

I was two feet away. I felt unworthy, and I was worthless. Her casket was cold, and the cold crept into my soul. Exiled on desolate lands.

I had to look. I had to say my goodbyes. "Mom, I loved you, I will miss you, and I just don't know why."

She was wearing a white dress; it was something simple from her closet that was chosen as my mother's favorite. Her long brown hair was combed smoothly and rested down the front of her body just past her shoulders. She did not have any jewelry on, as usual, except her wedding ring that she never took off.

My most significant mistake was her hand. I touched it. Ice froze my pumping blood. It felt hard. It wasn't her.

I felt awed and dumbfounded. I pulled back, closed my eyes, and said my silent prayer. "Sweet dreams, Mom, in heaven. In the clouds. In God's needy arms."

I grew distant from God, from people in my own world. I wanted to pretend that everything was normal, that addiction hadn't consumed my mom. In a way, I'd known even as a small child that the avalanche would eventually take her away. So many days I had come home from school wondering if this would be the day, the day her lonely heart ceased to beat, the day her eyes just wouldn't open. I had often felt anguish inside as I left for school, feeling twisted knots of confusion as I waited for the bell. The walk home had been full of crippling fear.

As I sit here writing, my perceptions are shifting. I feel light penetrating my soul, her beautiful hands guiding my pencil. For so long, I merely blocked her and her angelic hands. As I said in the beginning, she was an angel in a wicked world and lonely on an island of darkness. She tried her hardest; she really did. This I will say as my soul is opened up, "Mom, I forgive you. I promise! So smile down with the pain emptied out. You're amazing. You're in heaven's hands. Enjoy it. You deserve the infinite river of bliss."

Chapter Thirteen

Christmas and Smiles

Winter's leaden skies came, the crispness of the air confirming the time of year. Flakes of snow fell, and the ground was sprinkled with a thin layer of the clouds' oppressive weight. I stood at the window in front of the sink, inspecting winter's beauty

We had stayed with Gram's after Mom's funeral, fighting for some ordinary routines. Healing proved difficult for us, but day by day, we moved forward.

I felt excited to set up the Christmas decorations. This was my favorite holiday with strings of lights blinking, the Christmas tree's radiance healing, and the unity of family in a sea of love.

The Christmas decorations and the tree were stuffed in the attic. Its entrance was centrally located between the two bedrooms at the back of the house. Built from plywood, the attic had a door that swung down to rest against the walls. We had to get out an aluminum ladder to gain access.

The tree was held in garbage bags, each color-coordinated limb size was separated from the other. We moved furniture around to make the tree fit in the living room, taking some out. Flurries of stimulating energy flew about.

I felt the pull of the world attempting to anchor me down, but the love that surrounded me, saintly and pure, persuaded me to surrender to my grandma's sure will.

Christmas songs were playing, snowflakes descending, and sugar cookies were thrown on the counter. Gram taught us how to bake, each step including preheating, making the dough, and rolling it out.

Once again, she examined our hopelessness, took her brilliant Band-Aids, and did her best to bind our childlike innocence inside.

I love Christmas. I learned so much from Gram. Her warmth was something I cherished. The smells filling the air, the way she laughed, and the way she saw into my soul. Her special embrace, her simple light, and I will never forget her willingness to accept us as hers. Being in her presence altered me. Her light brightened my flitting shadows, helped to hold me back from complete collapse. If it wasn't for her, I don't know if I would have ever felt human again. I would be soulless, put quite simply as Satan's robot.

We helped Grandma set up the Christmas tree, and my father happened to find us a place, so we moved with him before Christmas Day.

Dad rented us a new apartment out on Tortilla Flats. Everyone from Price calls it that, and it's a little over a mile from Grandma's house. It was a two-level set of apartments, and we lived on the upper floor.

Opposite the apartment were remnants of dead trees. Winter had absorbed all the green. Allissa was moving in with us. She would be a perfect addition to our little family.

On Christmas, the sounds of morning rustled me awake. My siblings stirred excitedly. Santa Claus had come, and bubbles of enthusiasm quickly woke me.

I regarded the love in this house, the togetherness, and thought of Mom on her soft white cloud. I was boiling inside from fury at her death, but I loved her and missed her fiercely. It was Christmas, and I wanted her with us.

We ran into Dad's room to wake him, but before that, we cheated and stole a quick glance at Santa's gifts in the living room. We only took a glimpse before the guilt hit, and we bolted out. We didn't even knock at Dad's door and just stormed right on in, the four of us. Dad shot right up, his smile cresting.

The living room warmed up when Dad kicked on the heat. We sat on the couches, sharing smiles and warm laughs. Each of us passed around gifts. Wrapping paper shredded instantly as joyful memories were created.

I felt ecstatic to be living with Dad. It was truly a blessing for all of us to be together, and I worked on blocking the shadows I carried.

I tried to see life for what it really is. I was shuffled and jaded, but among it all, I just wanted love. We were bound to each other, family. Hard steel. I honored the time we had together.

My dad's sorrow, which he pushed beyond, was obvious. He gaped at us with despairing love. You know the expression I am speaking of when tragedy has struck and the guardian has to stay strong for those around them. They wear a mask and say it is okay so the rest of us can heal. But beneath the porcelain mask, beyond the scars, lies agony, and I could sense it crawling beneath the surface.

Chapter Fourteen

Rifle Mastery

Life started to speed up after that. Different patterns formed in the unfolding of days.

Addiction has ways of leaving families broken, torn, and bleeding. Cycles expand farther and farther until something jumps in the way. I have seen so many inmates of all ages come in here who have been in this treacherous cycle. Addiction doesn't care. It destroys all that is pure and good.

I see the pain riddled in inmates' eyes as they lie trying to excrete the poisons, kicking and screaming. Again and again, they try to stay out of jail. But when their support system scatters, or their supporters are on drugs as well, they fall flat on their faces.

I'm not justifying mistakes. I am speaking from what I know, from the wisdom of living it. It's hard for people to desire sobriety when they ache inside, their parents are strung out, or their grandparents raised them.

I have asked many people the same questions, seeing their scars and knowing the viciousness. The answer is always the same. Why not use?

They feel worthless and lost, crushed and used up.

New life drew back for another year. Bulb flowers perked from their bed as the soil warmed and the sun's increasing light intervened. The freshness of lilacs breezed about, reminding the depraved world that there is still pleasure to be felt.

I stood among it all, taking it in. I was ready for spring's embrace. Today was going to be great. We had a full day planned out. Now I just had to wait for my dad's friend, Kevin, to get here.

I paced, the first one to wake, of course, with the thought of going shooting stirring inside me. Dad sat on the balcony, sipping a hot cup of coffee and enjoying the warm spring morning with a cigarette in his mouth.

Kevin pulled up in his old spray-painted Chevy truck with his son, Bean, by his side. Kevin sported a brimmed hat, and of course he had the mullet out the back. He and my dad had been best friends since childhood. They had experienced life united: girls, fights, parties, and skipping class.

Kevin had an energetic smile and laugh. When he was around, you felt it. If it was warm, he usually wore his signature cutoff shorts. He was like an uncle to us. When he and Dad were together, they both transformed. They had their own type of speech that had developed from years of perpetual closeness. He would call me Jessy Michael and continually ruff up my hair.

Bean was Kevin's son and reflection, and when we were all together, it was something to behold.

Sage scraped the side of the truck when we veered off the dirt road. Remnants of snow crushed beneath the tires. As I gazed out the camper shell windows at the snowcapped mountains, I felt glad I'd brought my winter wear. The guns lay in the rack behind the seat, and music flowed out the rolled-down windows. Dad and Kevin cheerfully smoked.

We all loved Bean. He was a year younger than me, and he would look just like Kevin when he became a man. We loved how the cedars' smell carried in the air as we fished, and how the poles shook when we hooked our scaly rewards.

I was lost in the distance when I heard gunfire. My head swiveled to the cab. I found Dad loading the .22. We had stopped so Kevin could shoot out the window. A little gray rabbit narrowly made its escape, jumping and hopping farther away.

When we started moving forward again, Dad held the butt of the rifle on his lap, the barrel leaning out the open window.

They hunted like this throughout my life; rock and roll music was playing: the Eagles, Lynyrd Skynyrd, or Black Sabbath. The love of their music ventured through us, embedding notes in the canyon of our scars. When a certain song plays, still to this day, it takes me back to a place and time. Smells of cigarettes, wide smiles, and laughs.

Dad and Kevin walked to the other side of the ravine. This is where they set the bag of bottles, glazing the distance with the bottles' translucence.

We took our positions. I lay on the snow, the butt of the rifle resting on my right shoulder, the ground holding me stable, my breath an act of natural finesse. Pop, breathe, shoot. One target shattered. Expel casing, reload shell, breathe, focus, and pop. Such a gliding pattern.

I was good with a rifle. It came so naturally to me as if I'd been born with it in my hand. Yeah, I was young, but I understood the entire procedure of shooting. Lining up the sight with the bead, breathing calmly, and resting on something stable. Dad only had to tell me once. It was second nature.

Jeremy didn't shoot yet since he was only five. Kenny was nine and as good as me. His brown hair shone underneath his hat. Taking the small pump-action rifle from me, he replicated the same movements

Dad had taught us. Each shot of the rifle found its mark. Glass splintered and echoes rang as the gun smoke dispersed in the cool air.

Recalling events of that day brings forth a joy equal to nothing I have ever experienced. The black-and-white spray-painted truck, Dad's and Kevin's behavioral switches, and the smell of sulfur spent in the lively air.

My cell door is locked, and bricks encase me. This stool I am sitting on is hard, and I sit here doubting myself. My intent is for my story to help you see the quakes that addiction causes. There is no true consistency. Pain wraps around everyone involved like a spiderweb.

It's hard to believe in myself. It always has been. I pray for my story to be seen by all because if it is not, it feels as if it was all for nothing. There has to be a reason why I remember all of this, why I see it so clearly.

For years, I blocked it. But after the suicide attempt, the tight sheet around my neck, and losing complete consciousness, I felt the shift while sitting on suicide watch. I was there for what seemed like years when it was actually only twelve days with nothing but a padded Velcro suit, no mattress, no toilet, no books or pencils, but worst of all, no human contact. Something snaps when you tear down like that. My hair went gray, my mind raced, and finally I brought everything from my past back up from the cave.

Life is beautiful; it really is. The smiles, the laughs, and even the hardships. With pain comes strength. Layer upon layer it grows. Inside it all, though, are scars, deeper, longer, and bordering on maddening.

I've cried tears of the heaviest weight, burning like fire, and what seemed to be deprived of all life. I couldn't pray. I tried, but something blocked it. I felt soulless, wicked, and unworthy of God's grace.

My angels from above saved me from hell's gates. Believe me, we all have them. They're there when you almost slam into a car head-on or cross a crosswalk and narrowly miss being hit. It's a simple hand, graceful, transparent of all humanly form. A nudge, a silent whisper, and you are compelled from entering the beyond.

Chapter Fifteen

Drunken Stupor

It was getting hot that summer, and I yearned for cooler days. We stayed inside where it was cooler, and Alissa had a few friends over when Dad wasn't home. We watched *Children of the Corn* (yeah, I know, a little intense for kids). During certain scenes, I covered my eyes, but the sound of the killing still ate at me. I remember having very specific nightmares about children standing malevolently, staring into fields of corn as I ran and got lost through endless rows with seemingly no escape.

When the movie ended, I woke up Bear and helped waddle him to bed. Ken and I were going to stay up with Alissa and her friends. I sat in the recliner, coloring and listening to the crickets chanting outside, protected by the shade of the night.

In the kitchen, Alissa and her friends were drinking and having fun. Ken had the TV turned on to some Disney cartoon.

I was drifting further into the sounds when I heard footsteps stumbling up the front steps. I honestly didn't think anything of it. One step, two steps, stop, three steps, stop, and then he fumbled in the front door.

He had brown hair, seemed tall, had a protruding gut, and was naked from the toes up. He stood there, a statue of nude drunkenness and perversion, slurring and wobbling, calling out for my sister.

I recognized this man. He was the neighbor from downstairs. Now, though, he seemed to be a different person.

He was at least my dad's age. He held his penis in his hand and played with it. He came farther inside. All of us were shocked. We didn't know what to do; it all happened so fast.

My feet were planted to the floor, my body rigid as stone, and my eyes fixed ahead. Off in the distance, I saw a set of headlights.

Dad saw from the car what was transpiring. Its door sprang open, and he flew. I really would have hated to be that drunken fool.

Dad's footsteps felt like aftershocks, and I knew this wasn't good. When you live in addiction's wake, you never call the police. We were raised to never trust them, honestly. I don't think we even knew to call 911.

Dad pushed the neighbor by the throat into the open door. It flew back, splintering into pieces. The man hit the floor, writhing in a drunken stupor. Dad helped him to his feet by the back of the neck and hair and not-so-elegantly helped him down the stairs.

Once they hit the grass pad below, Dad laid into him. I thought he was going to break the man into two. Dad just kept on beating. When he finally stopped, he got the man up and begrudgingly helped him to his apartment.

That was a night I will never forget. How disgusting the man was, the vileness of what he said, and how he motioned to Allissa. I found it appalling on every level. It reminded me of the time I had been molested.

I also started to see how I was like Dad in my rage. How time seemed to stop, air cracking, and his total transformation in character. You could actually feel the energy surrounding him.

What lasted a total of maybe three minutes seemed like hours. Dad's compelling force was scary as he demolished the man, each smack of the fist, the way he grabbed his neck and kicked his ribs.

I was just a kid, but to see this violence engaged shadow memories of Dad's fight with Mom. The way Dad held her down and struck her as she pleaded to be let go. The way his rage, her screams enclosing us, hell's wrath breathing, and bells of sorrow ringing.

Chapter Sixteen

New Beginnings

Tracy, or "Aunt Tracy" as I called her, lived on the east side of Price. She is my dad's first wife and mother to Allissa. I used to love going over there. We would have huge amounts of ice cream bars, pop ups, and every other kind of ice cream snack possible. We watched movies, new ones, on a large TV. We all ran around doing what we wanted. With the addition of Alissa's two half sisters, we were a bunch of ice-cream-eating hoodlums.

We went to Tracy's frequently to see Allissa after she moved back to her mother's and blithely play in the backyard. She had a remarkable playhouse. It had a ladder that led up to a loft and a slide that gracefully brought you back down. Attached to the other side was a swing, and sand encircled the entire structure.

I started noticing a shift in Dad's behavior. I would get up late at night, and he would still be up. When he did sleep, it would be at odd hours.

When we went to Tracy's, the parents would go into Tracy's bedroom and do their thing although at the time I couldn't fathom what that was.

I noticed unnecessary movements in the adults' arms and legs, overemphasized wiggles and shifts as they spoke. And their eyes were everywhere, taking in everything in the surrounding environment.

Weird people were around whom I had never seen before, doing the same thing, trying to sit calmly, but fighting to hold still. There were cigarettes everywhere in ashtrays, lying there smoking but none being held. They would light them and forget they were there, but the smoke was everywhere. They would start on a specific project, cleaning or fixing something with enthusiasm, hands moving a million miles an hour. Then, halfway through, they would jump to something else.

I had to pay great attention to what was transpiring, being sick of having my heart in a vise. I felt sure that staying on my toes was an act of survival. Vigilance was the key. I tried to protect myself from the darkness drawing around me.

Meth addicts carry a certain morbidity with them wherever they go. They have either been up too long, days fading away, or sickness whispers in their twisted minds. Their bodies take the appearance of being undernourished with cheeks sunken in, eyes hollow, and lifeless. They wander with no direction and often wires and weird electronics scattered everywhere. They break perfectly functioning things to pieces in order to put them back together. The whole time, they think that they are actually super intelligent gadgeteers when in reality, they are sleep-deprived idiots floating somewhere between heaven and hell. Dad met Leesa during this tumultuous timeframe.

My nine-year-old heart had a difficult time sorting between what was reality for us and normal for others. On TV, I saw the shows *Family Matters* and *Full House*. I saw the way they had set times for dinners and sat about spending quality time together. Everyone had his or her specific family role. They laughed and cried so innocently. They faced normal family hardships like loss of work or a boyfriend or girlfriend. When I looked at our disfigured normalcy, I began to see that normal was an illusion.

Whack! I got hit in the head with a pair of rolled-up socks. Brittany laughed, her facial features sharp. Her brown hair spun as she followed through with the throw. Dad was upstairs with Brittany's mom, Leesa, and my brothers and I were downstairs playing sock war with Brittany and Ethan.

Jeremy grabbed hold of a pair and hucked it at Ethan, smacking him in his five-year-old round face. Jeremy was fighting tears. We all laughed as the night wore on.

Brittany and Ethan were brother and sister but were strikingly opposite when it came to physical appearance. Ethan's ears were bigger than Brittany's. He was chunky, and she was slim. Brittany was seven, and she had a sporty energy whereas Ethan was even more timid. We were having a blast until Ken nailed Ethan hard in the face with his pair of socks. Tears flowed, and we all fought to hush the wailing that poured forth. We knew we had to quiet the crying.

Methamphetamine hit the town of Price like a plague that year. Everywhere we went, people had pick sores torn on their faces and arms. We frequented places I had never been before. House after house seemed plagued by meth vengeance. People "zipping," scattered and lost in a world of inflated confusion. Yards packed with broken down cars, junk, and remnants of completely useless objects designed to appease their owner's overcrowded minds.

The blue apartments where we lived stood two stories high, and there were five buildings spread right by a marshy drop-off where small puddles of stagnant water lapped against cattails. In the sunny, sticky air, black-and-white magpies glided, surveying the lands.

We were once again in the nearly vacated town of Wellington, Utah. Dad and Leesa decided that it was time we lived together, and the three-bedroom apartment became our home. All the boys shared a room, the parents had theirs, and Brittany was given her own room, which was larger than ours, and *that* provoked irritation with me.

Adjusting to a new family proved to be bothersome. I had grown accustomed to our daily routine, knowing each other's moods, wants, and needs. Now I had to adapt to Brittany's frequent tantrums. Let me tell you, when she started in on a BritFit, lying on her back on the floor, her heels and balled-up fists hammering on the wood under the carpet, the pictures rattled on the walls. The noise, oh my, the sounds, made me want to run away.

I hated Leesa. I never wanted anybody to think that they could come sliding into my life and try to replace my mother. I was closed to the option of having a replacement, and that made me feel hatred toward her when her scornful hands tried to massage my scars from behind her smile that I felt was fake. I felt that my scars were mine that I protect and own, and I was not open to sharing the pain with her and just wanted her to stay away from them. My walls kept me safe in my world.

So I climbed farther into my cage, diluted by my own distance and swimming under black ice. I started to see favoritism emerge as Dad yearned to keep the peace. All four of us boys shared a room while Brit had hers with a king-sized bed and a mountain of brand-new toys.

I evaded everyone. I floated in my own world. When I built Lego, my shadows helped. When I played outside, my shadows played with me, and when I wandered the marshy lands, my shadows were the ones following.

As the meth-infused hands of time moved forward, I attempted to lower some of my defenses. Still, I feared that if I did remove the protective sphere, the creeping colorless world would slowly crush me.

Thankfully, my cousins lived a block away, and that is where I started to find some escape. Ken and I would go play with our cousins, Danny and Cody. Yeah, I'm speaking of my minion double and his brother who is Ken's age. We would wonder around the fields nearby and go on adventures as we would describe them, which would consist of shooting BB guns at bottles and seeing who could throw rocks the furthest and/or hit the targets we would place from a distance. Times like this would help me forget about my shadows. I would laugh, smile, run free, and feel free.

Chapter Seventeen

Pushing Limits

My father taught us to disregard those who were not of the white race. I was told to not trust "them" and never bring "one" home. By "them," he was usually referring to African Americans. He always said, "You can only trust them as far as you can throw them."

I was too young to understand the negative energy created by empty hate and the fact that you cease advancing spiritually when you hold onto hate.

It is a sinful habit that still claims many in the world, programmed by generation after generation, for whatever reason. I can't begin to understand why it is so prevalent, but I know the shadows it creates. We all do. Waves of loss, vicious deaths.

Mankind bleeds. We all hurt, and we love. We strive to be connected and seek comfort from one another.

I snuck up to our neighbor's door. My feet on the sidewalk sounded like beats on a drum, but in reality, they struck as light as a feather. The moon was mounted directly above as summer's night breeze wafted past me. Nervous sweat formed on my brow, and my hands were balled into fists.

Then I reached to ring the doorbell. It was nearly blinding. I took a breath, looked left and right, drew a little closer, and breathed in. Inches away, I felt my sweat crawling. With the thump of my heart, I pushed it. *Ding-dong.* And I bolted.

My legs pumped little pistons as I fled as fast as I could. Danny's giggles flew through the air. We would run into the field near the apartments and laugh even though it felt so nerve-racking at the same time. It was a rush.

The door flew open, and I found a bush by the marsh to use for cover. I sat on my butt and held my knees to my chest and peeked through the slim limbs and leaves. A tall man with short gray curly hair turned his head and headed toward me. The moonlight beamed down, piercing and jeopardizing me. I tried to slow my breathing.

Then I caught the glare. Resting in his hands laid a long gun. It swayed, barrel pointing down as he stomped closer and closer. I wanted to shut my eyes but forced them to stay open.

This man was furious, and I knew it. He cursed and used vulgar language and cruised forward. The sigh of wind felt cool, brushing my sweat.

My body was as rigid as stone when he found me. If I had tried to move, my departure would have rattled his senses. So I sat there, silent and scared.

He seized me by my shirt collar, dragged me out of the bush, and threw me to the ground. I looked up and stared into the tubes of a double-barrel shotgun.

Fear froze me. I tried to speak but couldn't find the words. It felt like my throat had closed up, and the whole world around me jumbled into a knot of trembling gloom. My eyes watered as he cursed loudly, implying he should just blow my head off.

My fear heightened when I heard the desperation in his voice. His gun shook, and his hazel eyes were teary. I thought I was never going to see my Dad or my brothers again, that they would lose me, and hell was finally coming to swallow my scarred soul.

Pee ran down my legs as he jabbed me on the top of my head with the barrel. He raised the gun from my head, turned the other way, and as he walked away, he mumbled, "Never do that again or else."

This is the first time I have ever told this story. The only other person who knows about it is Danny. I was embarrassed to tell anyone because I had peed my pants, but mostly I didn't want the confrontation. I was scared that my dad would kill the old man for pointing a gun at me or even get shot himself.

Some lessons are harder to learn than others. I never went doorbell-ditching again, but throughout my life, I constantly added more and more to what I like to call my "karmic web."

Each tiny filament of the web grew and expanded to build a form of energy around me. This is caused by the choices that I made throughout my life. I carry this energy everywhere. It is part of me, composed of light and darkness. The choices that caused the positive and negative energy that formed my web.

This is why it's important, in my beliefs, to build a loving web around myself. A web of forgiveness, gratitude, and integrity. We can just go through the motions in life—living, eating, and making money—but what really matters is who we are behind closed doors.

Are our thoughts pure? Do we lie? Do we cheat and steal? What do we do with our spare time? Do we help or hinder? Do we look at one another with love in our hearts? What do you think when you see a vagrant on the side of the street?

All of this truly matters. It becomes our web. So strive for love, be light, and see life through the eyes of true integrity. Your web is strong, and it follows you everywhere. So dig deep and really ask yourself who you truly are. That's the path to enlightenment in my eyes. Knowing who I am. No matter when or where or who else is around.

Chapter Eighteen

Cigarettes and Skinny Dipping

My legs were soaked to my knees as I fought hard to take one more step forward. The tough marshy mud held on, like a suction cup, nearly pulling off my shoes. The smell of the inert water wafted through the hot air. Mosquitos zipped around, thriving on the blood I annoyingly provided.

I peered to my left and saw that Ken and Cody were already several paces ahead, the sound of the mud and water slurping with each step. Danny struggled behind me, his young voice cursing at the difficulty of our adventure.

We came to the end of the swamp near our house and strutted up the slick bank to the dry grass at the top. Trees were scattered slightly ahead, and all I could look forward to at this point was the luxury of shade. I was beat. Sweat poured from my head down my back, and the smell of the swamp mud clung with a vengeance. I sat on an old log and wiped the sweat off my face with my shirt.

We pushed on, stepping over branches, bushes, and puddled water. We were exploring all-new territory for some unexpected treasure. We had no objective. We were just being boys and were delighted in what lay undiscovered. When we came to a clearing, I heard water flowing in the distance. I knew it was a river; this would cool us down and clean the nasty smell.

A few animal skeletons lay camouflaged by the dead weeds. In the clearing were abandoned shells of assorted rusted vehicles. They were old and were completely stripped.

We all sat on top of an old truck. Tree branches leaned over us, and the breeze in the shade felt great. Cody had brought a pack of cigarettes, and I was excited to smoke one. Maybe, this time, I could smoke one all the way down. I had tried smoking before when I was younger, burning ones left in the ashtray. I had hacked, almost puking, and now I had to impress the boys.

I took a cigarette from Cody's extended hand, smiling, and he handed me the lighter. The two older boys were already puffing away on theirs, but Danny waited for me to light mine.

Dad always held it at the right of his mouth as he lit one, cupping the lighter. Packs rolled up in sleeves, giant arms bulging, and cool men wearing cowboy hats and riding horses all flashed through my mind.

So I put the Marlboro between my lips and struck the lighter, gracefully blocking the air that flowed past, and took a drag. I was careful to only inhale a little bit. I had learned my lesson. I wanted to look like a real cowboy. Better, I wanted to look like my hero.

I got halfway through the burning stick, gaining some momentum, and starting to inhale little by little. I held it perfectly between index and middle finger down to my middle knuckle.

That is what makes a smoking man look tough, how he holds his smoke, where he positions it in his lips, and how he exhales it. All this mattered, making me one tough, good-looking cowboy.

I lay on my back, closing my eyes, sick, and trying to regain some control over the spinning world above me. The others laughed and asked if I was going to be okay.

The heat helped saturate my already sweating body, and the weeds poked through my soaked shirt, making me itch. If this is what it took to smoke, then I vowed to never touch a cigarette again.

But, of course, that didn't work out how I planned.

The strength of cigarettes has haunted me for years. I have tried to quit on my own using patches or gum. Unfortunately, that only ever assuaged my desire temporarily.

It's something about the hand movements, the routines built around smoking. Sitting on the front porch with the sun rising into the morning sky, coffee in one hand, Marlboro in the other, enjoying that simple moment before the beat of a dreadful day.

Now that I am telling my story, I understand how critical it is for me not to follow the paths I have always followed, the winding path of thorns and hidden traps.

Every choice I make, every thought, every action builds my web. When I know what is wrong and I go against it, the cycle starts. Small shadows form. No one sees them, but before long, everyone around me gets pulled into my twisting anarchy. Looking up to others and trying to be like them can cause me to fall into a trap that I knew is destructive. I destroyed them, yet I still followed in their steps.

Chapter Nineteen

One Day a Spelling Bee

Dad and Leesa decided that it was time to move. There just weren't enough jobs in Wellington. They found a three-bedroom, one-and-a-half-bath condo to rent. It would be the nicest place I had ever lived.

I remember being upset when we set up the two sets of bunkbeds that we would sleep in. Brit got her own room again, which, of course, was bigger than ours. My envious young mind grew agitated. I didn't have the ability to separate my thoughts from what was really happening, that my Dad's intent was to keep Leesa happy.

I felt angry, hurt, and confused. I slipped further into my hole.

The school year had barely started; I was in third grade. I remember my teacher clearly. She had shoulder-length red hair with tinges of gray starting around her ears. Her nose was large, and she always wore long dresses with flower prints.

She had a different style of teaching. Each morning started with lessons in stretching, and one day each week, she taught us parts of the

Japanese language. We listened to books on tape. It was like watching a movie while sitting at my desk.

I started to write a book about a kid who goes on these tremendous adventures, facing all kinds of adverse circumstances. I still remember the simple plot with my main character jumping trains and wading through swamps.

My teacher really loved me. She spent extra time explaining things in detail. I asked her lots of innocent questions. She fed my young brain, and I soaked it up. She still has a special place in my heart to this day. I will never forget her.

There is no true consistency. By this time, at the age of nine, we had already moved six times that I remember. In each place, I had to acquaint myself with new territory. So I learned not to get close to people. It was easier this way. Developing friendships and having sleepovers didn't exist. I hung with my brothers although I started to bring Leesa's kids close to my protective bubble.

I brought my homework home, trying to learn and advance my mind. No one had to twist my arm or push me into my studies. Grandma's saintly routines had trained this into me. Her constant reminders of the need for an education in this world, and her loving knowledge of raising children, still flows through me.

My spelling was advancing, and I grew hungry for harder words. My teacher saw this and pushed me. She challenged me, and it aroused foreign areas of thought I had never known existed. For years, I had been forced to believe I was trash, that I was not good for anything, but she coaxed me to believe differently. Her tactic worked.

I started writing words over and over, training myself and preparing for the school spelling bee. The fear I felt was almost crippling. I did not want to fail. One of the main reasons why I had never challenged myself before was because of the possibility of failure.

I feared standing in front of everyone, their eyes observing me, waiting for me to crumble in front of them. I imagined sweat forming as they waited for the next letter and trying to remember while my heart beat hard. Is it an "*I*" or an "*E*"? I feared spitting out the wrong letter and passing out as the audience all pointed and laughed.

I still studied every day, but I hid it. I didn't want family to come to the spelling bee and see my failure, so I said words to myself in the bathroom or wrote words alone in my room.

When I tried to look at myself in the mirror, it was so difficult. My teacher told me to stand in front of it and repeat words, so I tried. Standing there, spelling them out; I tried to maintain eye contact. It didn't work well with me. I had built a system of bathroom procedures over time. Never look myself in the eyes. Gaze to the left or right, brush teeth, fix hair, don't look at the forehead. It was difficult to look at myself with the self-hate running below the surface. So I sat on the toilet, sticking to my system, and I threw my teacher's advice out the window.

When the time came for the spelling bee, I was nervous. I could hardly sleep the night before. Letters ran in front of my mind. Laughs haunted my dreams. When I woke up, I had sweaty palms. Today was the big day. So I got out of bed and went to the bathroom. I did my normal routine and also ran over some words in preparation. I wanted to pound them into my skull. I simply could not fail. It was not an option.

The walk to school always felt fearful. The sun peeked over the beautiful Rocky Mountains, and I saw fire in the skies. On the whole way to school, I told myself, "You are worthless. Why are you even trying? You will fail, you are trash."

In the classroom, I took my seat, and my teacher looked over at me with a warm smile. I wanted to run, but I had to do this. I wanted the chance to do something good despite my fear.

As the swelling waves of anxiety expanded in my stomach, I remained focused on winning. This would be the day I will not succumb to my weakness.

The podium provided little cover from everyone's eyes. I sat on the stool shaking. I was glad my family had not come then they would not be able to see me fail. I closed my eyes, sweat dripping, and feeling like an idiot forever thinking I could compete. I felt angry with myself, angry with my teacher.

Trash! Trash! Trash! I thought as the spelling bee official asked me my first word. I drifted through tunnels of torment as I forced each letter, trying to focus on getting it right.

Next thing I heard was clapping. What the hell? Never in a million years had I thought I would hear that. It was for me! My heart grew lighter, and Grandma's proud smile flashed in my mind.

Lights pierced my shadowed self, waiting for the wind to pick me up like dust and blow me away. I held onto the podium, word after word. More applause, more beautiful music to my soul. Every clap was like a pat on the back, and it felt delightful.

Finally, three people remained. Letters were spoken, ripping through the auditorium's air. I knew that when they gave me a complex word, I would take third. Which was fine. Third place was just as good as first to me.

The next word that I was given was "potential." That was as far as I made it, and I was unable to successfully spell it. Smiling from ear to ear, I wore my third-place ribbon proudly thinking, "I did it!" I marched off the stage hugging myself, feeling proud.

The power of affirmations will never change. You are what you tell yourself. Throughout my life, the indestructible force of my self-talk had shackled me. There I remained, wading in harmful patterns of anguish and absent of all forms of essential love.

I'd never worked through or accepted hardships; I buried them. I turned them into a phantom created by my own misunderstanding. *Must be my fault,* I told myself. I'm wicked or unloved for some ungodly reason.

That is why I force myself to stare into my eyes, to see who resides in the reflection. Who I am deep in my soul. I am enduring, kind, and compassionate. It is now in my control to create a life full of joy. Life no longer has to be volatile because I tell myself who I really am.

Every single day is a challenge. I pray for the strength to tell myself I am worthy of self-love. When the screams of darkness try to rain power over me, I close my eyes and put myself in that perfect, tiny blue house amid smells of Rave, pancakes, and Grandma's sweetness. I listen and feel the pulse of her love, her guiding light, her huge callused sunspotted hand wrapping around mine. I hear her saying, "Jessy, it is time to live. It is time to love yourself. You are worthy. You're perfect just the way you are."

Look at yourself in the mirror. Who do you see? Honestly. Do fears run beneath the surface buried by ego's lies? What are you scared of?

Start to sift through those fears, lies, and the self-talk. Love yourself because you're beautiful, not because of your accomplishments.

You have so many heavenly traits. Laughs that help others heal. A simple touch that warms a soul. And when you tuck your child in at night, you're wrapping them in a web of security that transcends everything physical.

It doesn't matter if you're a PhD, a teacher, or if you work at a tire shop. Love is love; it is separate from ego. That is what life is about,

what makes us beautiful, regardless of our mistakes or perceived weaknesses.

Chapter Twenty

Gossip and an Old Man

The Spanish Fork mountains were painted orange, stretching their rocky points endlessly into the crisp autumn sky. The air rolled down the slopes with a brisk touch, a reminder of winter's imminent arrival.

Dirt roads wound along the mountains and down to the small town of Spanish Fork. The land was varnished in green as the fields and trees reigned over the world they lived in.

Everyone played their part in a life untouched by digital civilization. There were miners, carpenters, farmers, blacksmiths, and general store workers. The perfect blend of social grace. People waved when they passed each other on the street, smiling, and being truly altruistic. Life was simple. But even in a simple world, evil crept, sneaking around like a light smoke caught in a skimpy wind.

I sat in a hard plastic lawn chair, shielded from the crispness with a sweater. My breath was visible as I stared at a house in the distance. A grumpy looking old man with messed up hair and a wrinkly face was standing out front, smoking a pipe and providing fear for all the neighborhood children to throw around in their childish stories.

One of the neighborhood kids told me the old man's story when he noticed the confusion on my face while trying not to stare at the him. He explained to me that the old man lived happily married with a young son who loved to fly kites in the sea of blue.

On a warm summer morning, the young man, possessing a strong back and fresh smile, was in the pasture tending to the normal daily chores. His beautiful wife and child had gone down to the general store for a few items, mostly to get out of the house and spend some time embraced in each other's company.

An old white house stood off the side of the road, bordered by alfalfa fields. Ahead stood a man dressed in coveralls, sweat washed down the front. Teeth were missing in his crooked smile. The smile screamed "run" as the mother and son approached him.

The mother grabbed her young son's hand, the quiver of fear racing through her as she attempted to stroll by. The man fumbled on his words, pulled out a large red revolver, and aimed it at her.

She could see by his slow movements that he was drunk; she struck out, attempting to disarm him. The gun fired.

Blood covered her dress as she fell to her knees, reaching out for her scared son. The boy screamed and looked from his mother to the shooter. The gun stared him in the face as the man pulled the trigger. Later, the shooter turned the gun to himself.

In a day when sweet birds sang merrily, flowers bloomed, and people loved, one man lost his wife and son to the wickedness of this world.

When the husband found out what had happened, his screams rang in complete agony. Bound by loss, he went mad, and he lived as a captive in his empty home. Lonely and scared, the man was flung into a hell he never returned from. He never went out to the store for supplies, never came out to the pasture, and his mail kept piling up.

One by one, his pigs disappeared, then his horses, and at last his two loving dogs.

Rumor was that he would come out at night to venture around town and snatch animals to feed on. Cats disappeared, dogs vanished, and if you came out when the moon stood high in the sky, you just might see him; his large coat hanging, limping slightly, with a sack over his back that held a cat or some other neighborhood animal.

During the day, he stayed locked in his dark house, cooking his find, making a sweet cat stew or canine steaks. Children believed that on days when he couldn't find an animal to eat, he would swipe an innocent child and throw them into his cauldron of death. As I said, "childish stories."

The vision streamed in my mind as the autumn air brought me back to the moment. I had heard bits of some tales at school and some through my siblings, all twisted and varying. My imagination twirled in its own creation of events, and before long, the man and the old house stood menacing as a night out of a horror movie.

Honestly, I didn't know what to believe as I gazed at the hunched old man. Parts of me were scared. Mostly, though, I felt tremendous bouts of guilt for retelling the childish gossip.

So before I knew it, my mind was made up. My heart was committed, and with my cold little hands stuffed in my pockets, I started toward the old man. I was no longer going to judge based on gossip. He deserved the benefit of the doubt. Perhaps he was just all alone in a world gone dark. Step by step, I grew nearer. Leaves tumbled, scraping the pavement as the smell of his sweet tobacco skimmed my senses.

His voice was raspy, marred by years of pipe smoke, and it sent a shudder down my spine. He looked directly at me and asked, "What do want?"

The way his voice cracked and the grumpy look on his face made me feel like I was just bothering him.

I dug deep, searching for an answer, any answer. I should have thought of a viable excuse prior to sauntering over to disrupt his reverie. Unfortunately, I had to seek out something buried by bricks of fear.

Quickly, I figured that the truth would be best. Forcing the lumps in my throat away, my voice squeaked up. I mumbled that I was curious about him. I said to him that everyone feared him, and I wanted to know more. The bottom line is I wanted to know the truth. I wanted to know his real story, and I wanted to get to know him.

My answer brought a warm smile, and I knew then that this man was no cat killer. He was merely living in a world of his own creation, in which wisdom had outlived ignorance.

With my fear and anxiety deflated, we sat on his porch. He told me simple stories of the past with his pipe in one hand. He would strike a wooden match after the glow of tobacco died and puff hard again, pulling life into the bowl. With each puff, one eye would scrunch shut and half of his face squeezed with it. When he spoke, half of his face was lazy, leaning toward the earth.

I learned that years ago, the love of his life had died of a heart attack, and after his heart snapped, he decided it would be useless to try to fill the void. Many people would be hurt if he tried to show false love, so he stayed alone, missing his high school sweetheart when the cycle started anew with each day.

He had two children which he held very close to his heart and ached daily to see. The retrace of life had pulled them away from him, making it rare for them to be together.

I easily felt the pain this aroused. He hid it with a wave of the hand, an act of being detached, but in his eyes, the strain of loneliness reflected off the tears he fought back.

When he changed the subject, he lifted his hand and pointed inside the house from which a lovely sweet smell erupted. The front door stood open behind a screen door. The screen door window was cracked. The scent of his spent smoke, added to whatever was inside, created a little piece of the divine in a world where loneliness multiplies with the changes of tides.

He stood up from the wicker chair, reached for the cane leaning against the wall, and shuffled toward the entry. He wanted to show me what he did with his time, he said, so I trailed behind him.

The screen door creaked open, and I got blasted hard in the face with the aroma of candy. Beyond the living room, the kitchen was heavily illuminated. As we approached the kitchen, I saw a huge machine, which he explained was his popcorn popper.

I inspected the living room. Old carpet lay underfoot, and pictures covered the walls. The furniture had the smoky orange look of a forgotten style. Overall, the house had a feeling of comfort, and I felt completely at ease in the home of someone I did not know, as foolish as it was.

The kitchen counters were all covered with plastic; the island in the kitchen held the popper, and on the other counter stood baskets holding wrapped popcorn balls. *So this is what he does,* I thought. After all the gossip of possible evilness dwelling in this warm home, it was a simple caramel popcorn ball manufacturing facility. Everything looked clean and tidy. Labels were stacked by orders already filled to meet the store's demand. One of the other counters was layered with wax paper and littered with caramel-covered apples.

My stomach grumbled. He saw this, plucked a caramel apple off the paper, and handed it to me with a crooked smile.

The hunched old man taught me two great lessons: First, gossip created fear, and fear kept the old man lonely. Every day when children walked by, he had to feel the stares, which added to his loneliness. I learned the truth of the greatest cliché ever. I had heard it before, but now I had actually seen and used it. "Never judge a book by its cover."

Even greater than that, I vowed right then to never let life get so ahead of me that I don't visit my father when he gets older. I knew, even as a child, that he would be alone in years to come. His first love had died, leaving a hole in his heart. Beyond his scars lay the impossibility of a fulfilling relationship.

My nine-year-old heart saw the effects of loss in others and how it applies to everyone. Love is powerful, love is beautiful, love spreads like wildfire.

Second lesson, always love, never give up, know that we all experience pain. Also, remember when you're sitting at home that your parents are thinking about you, wondering where you are, and what you are doing. They are remembering you laughing as a child, screaming, and running around in your diaper.

Those moments are forever seared in their memory. They are part of their souls, and always will be. So never give up on them. Don't let them sit at home alone, staring at the wall. Never take their love for granted.

Leesa really pushed to gain acceptance from my brothers and me. I saw Ken starting to allow her closer to him. They began to work on homework together and build a bond, a relationship that a son and mother would have.

I sat back with my shadows, keeping my cautious eyes scanning and searching for any reason not to trust her. What I found was a gentle flow of energy shared among the family. That was important but simple in my eyes, and something I had grown unaccustomed to because my past experience was my "normal." This is why I held onto my resentment so strong. No matter how messed up my family was before, it was mine. Everything that was happening now never felt right for me.

Ken was excellent in school. He drove himself hard in all of his studies. Perfectionism compelled him; he lived to do the absolute best. He was always organized, almost to a fault. I remembered I would move a few of his possessions around, instigating a shudder of complete terror.

Ken had no qualms about beating on me. I was his punching bag and his anger reduction tool, just as Bear was for me.

One day, Leesa and Ken sat at the kitchen table. Leesa had a typewriter out and was smashing keys, helping Ken with a project he was fixated on. His class was having a contest, creating a hardback book, and whoever won got it published. This stimulated Ken in an unhealthy manner. He couldn't see failure as a possibility.

Anyway, Leesa saw how important this was for him and dove in, opening her heart and helping in every way possible. Her smiles grew and her fingers flew.

I felt her desire to mesh herself into our lives. She only wanted the best for all of us, and my walls started to slowly tumble down.

I stood up from the stairs where I'd been sitting, scooting closer to the love I longed for. My heavy soul was ready to heal. Questioning everything in the path ahead was tiresome, but I still didn't oppose my need to do so. I just let some of my defenses down, to let some light into my soul.

Ken's book was called *Monsters in My Closet* and included amazing illustrations he'd created. He spent hours on this project. Constrained by timeframes, he charged forward. Leesa was there at every part of it, offering her creative impressions.

He was working on an essay for the book he had read. I was extremely proud and excited for the outcome of his hours of hard work. Ken's mental faculties were spread thin as the competition drifted nearer to completion. His fear was evident, and I often complimented his work.

When all was said and done after the judging, Ken won a second place title for his essay. He was proud. We all were. Humility was obviously intrinsic in our existence. The time spent writing, the love shared, the simple bonding showed virtue. This quickly reminded me of the way I felt when I took third place in my spelling bee. I knew how he felt and that made me so proud and gave me peace knowing that he got that same opportunity to feel that.

18-Wheeler

Dad's 18-wheeler was purple with orange flames running down the side. He began driving truck since we moved to Spanish Fork, and the balance in our lives advanced day by day.

Christmas passed, and the warmth outside grew brilliant. The sunshine and the Rocky Mountains during spring is remarkable with rays gleaming off the snow-washed mountains. Pine trees laced the natural phenomenon, and the tips of rock seemed to grasp for the sky.

I seized onto the side handle of my dad's wheeler, lifted my leg to the step above, and pulled myself into the cab. I felt like a king sitting on his throne, looking out the window as Dad gave Leesa a kiss goodbye. I waved to her, Dad hopped in his seat, and pride fluttered inside as Dad shot a wink at me. *This was going to be amazing,* I thought as the 18-wheeler roared to life. The gauges, buttons, and lever all told a story of complexity, reminding me of *Star Wars*, and I was the cocaptain of the ship.

Dad slammed the truck into gear after the brakes hissed their release. We started to move forward, my excitement mounting as the expert shifted through the path of gears.

The power I felt shaking through that hauling machine was astounding. I could actually feel it coursing through my body and to think that I was inside it on a mission with my dad.

Dad took complete control over the semi, hand on the wheel, gliding through gears with his foot dismounted off the clutch. He told me that the person who had trained him would tap him with a cane every time he insisted on using the clutch. He said that you have to feel the RPMs and shift when the truck is ready. Dad did this with efficiency. His skill was absolute. He flowed like a well-oiled, robotic truck-driving machine.

We turned onto the freeway. As our acceleration increased, huge green signs zoomed by. Dad had his window rolled halfway down, a Marlboro hanging out of his mouth, and his huge hand covered the gearshift handle.

It was a trip I will never forget. The brilliance of togetherness, a texture so smooth. This is what I had always longed for. The world seemed so drab in contrast to the excitement I felt with Dad. I was his second-in-command, gaining new experiences.

Off in the distant horizon, lay desolate white deserts, miles upon miles of salt, and to the right of us, the Great Salt Lake reflected beams of light. It seemed like an ocean to me as we drove the border of the salty mess. This was the first time I had been to this desolate waste.

On our first stop, we went to a restaurant just off of the freeway to rest, stretch, and eat. Our last stop was somewhere in Nevada. I had heard and read of deserts in school and seen the emptiness on TV, but to see it and press farther into the shell of land gave me a new respect for God's creation. It seemed as though the disquieting, bleak scenery would never end. Boredom started to tear at me, but I knew that it would not last forever.

Soon it ended, my heavenly voyage, stop after stop in our 18-wheel ship. Father and son traveling the world. My imagination expanded, and my young mind believed that we would never have to return to reality. But it came screeching to a halt as the air brakes were applied, the loud hiss echoing our trip's end. I glanced out the window. Our condo camouflaged our family, and I missed them all. Our little family had evolved, and our chain was getting more solid and consistent.

As I sit in my cell reminiscing, insights come. I enjoyed the time alone with my dad on that trip as new memories were made. It was then that I sincerely started to accept my new family. I missed them on our trip even though it was only one night. I had removed the barricades blocking their love just as they had. I missed Brittany's gap-toothed smile, Ethan's tiny laugh, and strangely, I missed Leesa's motherly ways.

We all knew that our parents were getting high. You gain a certain amount of perception when you grow up around addiction. Their moods were extreme, grating at our calm. My parents argued, locking themselves in their room for extended amounts of time. Before long, Dad lost his job, and the foundation we stood on crumbled.

Children are like sponges. They see everything around them, desiring love and comfort. It makes them complete, builds the foundation of the web that they will create for themselves when they start to make choices.

They can see the in-between, feel the energy flowing around them. When they see darkness and feel loneliness, they start to throw up walls. These walls keep their own light in.

As time passes and they think they can pull a brick out to look through, if they only see more pain, they build the walls stronger.

Fear becomes ingrained, part of their being. Somehow, they turn it on themselves, making the shadow's grasp their own fault. They swallow the vileness as their own.

It doesn't matter if you're an addict or not. Kids see all from provocative television commercials to simple arguments between parents. It stimulates regions inside their minds that they don't understand. Once the unknown erupts, they don't know what to do with it, so it's buried.

Chapter Twenty-Two

A Mountainous Home

D ue to my father losing his job again, the doors behind us in Spanish Fork closed, and the roads ahead were new. Summer had arrived, the school year was finished, and Dad bought a used motor home. This was where we would live for the summer, all six of us in a three-bed motor home. The motor home had one master bed and two large bunk beds with a divider separating the master bed.

We finally arrived at the new resting spot for our temporary home. We moved to Santaquin Canyon, Utah. All of us kids bounced off the walls with excitement. I opened the door and hopped out into the cool mountain air.

It felt like waves of heaven tenderly lapping my skin, and then I beheld the richness of the vision before me. Pine trees sheltered us at every angle, flying in the sky, blocking most direct sunlight. The smell was warm, piney, and rich with wildflowers.

To top it off, in the distance, I heard a squirrel chattering blended with a river flowing. The perfection was soothing, and my excitement to fish devoured my calm.

I pulled the metal stairs out of their recess, and everyone came tumbling out. Their impatience tore me away from my cloud in heaven. Their noisy voices floated about as they started to unwind the pent-up energy they held.

I was pulling out my fishing pole when Dad cut me off. He acknowledged my desire but informed me that I needed to help set up camp. So we set everything up, chairs, coolers, and a cool bug tent. I remembered going to the river for the first time. I stormed toward the sound of running water in the distance.

Dad had said that he would be right behind, and sure enough, I heard him yell my name as he jogged toward me, his huge 6'4" build bouncing.

We strode along together, the water pulling us closer with its notes. We took great strides as our excitement flared.

I gazed down, and the steady water in the holes reflected the sun's light. Immaculate holes with steady light swirling as the river's banks reached over the water. A fishing hole is a vision of flawlessness, a gathering of energy, a sight of simplicity blended with intricacy. Eating and living under the mingled knots of water were beautiful; scaly trout were lurking and eager to bite our lures.

Dad took the first hole, flipping his wrist, and planting his bait exactly where it needed to go. Each jig was adequate pressure, not too hard, not too soft. A mosaic of skills, traits born into him that often can never be taught. The fundamentals of fishing can be learned. But feeling the fish, knowing the water, the undercurrent, the banks and snags, that's in every molecule of a fisherman.

I took the next hole. Dad stood back, watching me mimic his movements. The water raced past, rivulets coursing. My keen eye observed every possible portion of the water. Precision is developed with practice, but I wanted to prove to Dad that I had the knack already, that I, too, was born with this natural ability.

I planted myself in a bank of moist grass. The water was maybe twelve feet wide, so I did an overhead cast with an open-faced reel. The lure hung from the tip no more than eight inches, providing ultimate control.

The breeze was perfect, and when I placed my spinner where I desired, I immediately started reeling. I cast upstream, bringing the bait along a shady bank so the light reflected off the chrome spoon.

I stayed patient, breathing calmly, knowing a fish would strike at any moment. Feeling the "in-between" provided the ultimate escape, where worries washed away in the current, pain was masked, and the only thing on my mind was the untainted moment of quiet.

Wham! Then the gold flash of underwater life struck. Vigorous muscles set the hook as the fish tore it underwater. My pole slammed down, bowing, shaking, and I started reeling vigorously.

Then the magnificent trout came flashing through the air. This was the vision of undeniable radiance that all fishermen seek. A curve of scales bearing colors, eternally sealed into the brain. Glimmers conceived in heaven as head and fins embraced the air the fish soared in. One divine instant in a life, on a riverbank, where addiction doesn't exist.

Living in the mountains that summer was adventurous. We produced memories that are embedded forevermore, the six of us entwined in the mountains' hold. I turned ten years old, fashioned in dirt and fires, marshmallow roasting, smoke rising, and stars covering us in the night.

We lived like this for a few months, fishing daily, hiking on the trails, and enjoying life outdoors. It couldn't last forever. We still had to go to school, so our parents found us another place to live, and yet again we moved.

One thing was constant: moving and living off instinct, rather than having a clear understanding. I came to understand that life is a constant change. Stability was forsaken. I survived by not forming attachments, by staying solitary.

Chapter
Twenty-Three

Smacks Ring
Louder

Our time in Spring Glen was tumultuous. Shadows of a fading night came roaring back from the chasm of our unsteady lives.

I sat on the couch upstairs playing Mario and watching him jump here and there, collecting coins. I remembered the sun was just starting to set for another span.

As my dad smacked Leesa's face, the sound shocked me. Shudders tore through me, cutting, seeming to vibrate through the walls.

I heard Leesa's piercing cries. My comfort fled as the screams rose. I continued to sit there, staring, trying to ignore what was occurring below me.

My hands felt melted to the control paddle. My siblings all possessed the same negative energy as I. We were struck by the fear of the fight. We all looked like we were filled with confusion, trying to understand exactly what we were seeing.

Slap, slap, slap. Echoes pillaged light as I moved down the steps, each step a canyon as I looked over the edge. I finally arrived at the bottom. The sounds were horrid. They slithered their way into my memory, leaving their mark.

I took a few more heavy steps to the end of the wall, peeked around the corner, and saw them lying on the floor. She was on her back as Dad held her down.

My dad was screaming at her as she screamed and begged him to stop. He kept yelling, "Why did you get into my stash?" With every scream and repeated question was followed by another hit making, an astounding sound of a slap. It seemed that with every strike, she was not even given the opportunity to ask his repeated question.

We were accustomed to not ever call the police; this was something that we were told that only caused more issues and was told that it would threaten our lives with our dad. We would be taken away; we would be put in homes with strangers. So because of this, the thought of calling the police did not even cross any of our minds, ever.

I gazed over, Dad saw me, and all of it immediately stopped. Shadows scurried out of sight, just like that, fleeing back to the pits where they had come from.

What I saw and heard that night was frightening. Abuse truly is tragic and unexplainable in its power.

It had seemed to take me forever to gain the courage to make it downstairs that far. I wish I could have stopped it sooner, but fear had frozen me. Guilt turned to shame for not acting. I felt sick to my stomach; it was in knots. I remembered going to the bathroom and fighting the urge to vomit.

I certainly didn't understand. I truly didn't know what to believe. I felt rotten, vile, gross, foul, and worse than all; I believed I was a coward. I should have done something sooner. Shame scared me, and I flew back into my shell.

The mirror reflected a figure of disgust, washed with magnified imperfections. I saw miles of forehead as a disfigurement. And to add to my self-hate, my buckteeth jutted out. I felt that I belonged in such an uncomfortable place and feeling even though in my own way it was comfortable. Eye contact with others became nonexistent.

I love my father more than I can put into words. He is and always will be my hero. The fact remains, though, that he created poisons that still floats inside me. It is as though there's an unseen wall of fog somewhere. But the anger and negativity I sometimes feel is hard to understand. My self-doubt, thinking I may not ever be able to succeed in life, sends me into an oblivion I simply don't comprehend.

I know that writing has helped tremendously. The poisons are etched onto the paper. I just feel that I am doing my dad a huge disservice.

I can't hold back any longer; I have to move through the filth. I still love him, but he was so severely lost in addiction that he could not be a dad. I have to face it to heal.

For years, I turned it into hatred of myself because I didn't want to hate him. It is now time to let go of the hate weighing me down and forgive the past.

Once again, Allissa moved in with us; we still lived in our house in Spring Glen, Utah; the parents still argued, but us siblings tried to look after each other although we still had our tense moments. Ethan and Bear stuck together, Ken was getting older and had his own friends, while I stayed to myself. Brittany, of course, had a slew of Barbie dolls to play with.

Allissa always seemed so much older than she actually was. She was sixteen in this part of the story, and I valued her reverent heart. She truly loved us all. Her abundant aura was so strong.

Agitated by the ups and downs, my realization set in greater than before. "Nothing will change. Expect the pain. Always be on guard." Expectations and hope seemed to be the epitome of evil in our world. So I lived without expectations.

I held a metal baking bowl in my hand. I was outside of the house by the camper. Inside the bowl lay a broken old digital clock, some batteries, and miscellaneous wire.

The warm air wrapped around me. Darkness swept the town, and the stars pierced down, a glimmer beyond explanation. These stars spoke to me with their twinkles, each separate blink a form of language. The breath of the sky seemed almost crystal. Small night clouds looked like gasses in space.

I made my way up the ladder connected to the rear of our camper, one hand holding the bowl, one holding a rung. One step up, wrap left leg, reach hand up, and continue until I reached the summit, the point in which I could set up a transmitter station.

The sounds around me were pleasing, a confluence of crickets chirping and leaves whispering, a reminder of nature.

I stood at the top, peering to the horizon. The book cliffs strove to be noticed. Alluring dark purples of the sky above bordered their cutting edge. Silhouettes of trees stirred in the summer's breeze, and in the distance, the lights of the power plant could be seen.

I didn't falter in my cleverness. Although my device couldn't possibly work, I made a willful attempt. I must have spent a couple hours on top of the trailer, lost in the dynamics surrounding me.

I didn't think about life at all. My spirit was wrapped in the world of imagination. The calm, beating heart of life at night absolved some of my torment. I peered through the clarity of the moment, pulling myself out of the corruption churning in a world where people were lost, floundering in their weaknesses.

I'd always believed that we were not alone in this universe. One of my favorite TV shows was *Fire in the Sky*. I reveled in the idea of being abducted and providing others with some information, hoping that I could make a difference on their planet.

I believed that there had to be a reason why the aliens snatched humans up, a reason other than basic experimentation. I thought they needed us to recreate their world and studied us to design a new race for their dying planet.

Chapter Twenty-Four

Lower Fish Creek, Utah

We got a dog from Uncle Troy. He was tan with brown spots and was as small as a chipmunk. I instantly fell in love. PJ was his name. He was sprightly; his run would turn into a hop as he neared me. We all loved PJ so much. The puppy ways brought joy into our hearts.

We were together every day. He followed us everywhere. When I went to school, PJ was all I thought about. I remembered my teacher got upset with me a few times due to my lack of focus. Everything I did was with him in mind. I fed him, I bathed him, and he slept in my bed. Cozy little ball of fur wrapped up beside me.

Our family started down the gravel road, laughter and love weaving through the car. Dad and Leesa sat in the front seat; all of us kids sat in the back. Our puppy hung out by our side.

We had one stop to make before we went camping to Lower Fish Creek, Utah. We had to stop at Grandma Peggy's house. I was stoked.

The motor revved as we descended south through Spring Glen and cut through our tiny town of Carbonville. Then followed Price, and Grandma's house came into sight, blue and beautiful. The memories I built in that warm, soft home I will never forget.

I felt proud to be taking Grandma with us. She had her stuff ready, and we began loading it. She didn't have much, so we were back on the road soon. The rest of the ride was gleeful, playing Uno and talking. We hardly felt the bumps and winding turns of the road. Spanish Fork Canyon towered high; Mother Nature's magnificence was apparent by the magnitude of its height and the forms of the rocky cliffs twisting above. God's artwork seemed to beam down as the canyon swallowed us.

I pushed down my hard demeanor, allowing the real me to shine through. My buckteeth poked out with each smile, each laugh, but it didn't matter. Gram was here, and I knew she only saw me, my enduring self. It showed with the passion in Gram's green eyes.

We turned onto the dirt road, the last stretch to my physical heaven. Scrub oaks covered the area around us, and the trail became a bumpy disaster. The motor home felt every rock, every jolt. Gram's white 'fro bounced. The smell of cigarettes wafted as Dad and Leesa puffed.

Dad took the turns slowly, methodically, but with each turn, the motor home leaned. Ravines from weather erosion rutted the road. He tried to miss most, but some he just had to push over.

We all pulled faces as we rolled through them. I held PJ in my hands. He didn't like the bumps. He hunched on my leg through the consistent rattling from the road.

We had traveled this road regularly throughout my life. There are points where you are separated by a couple feet of road from hundreds of feet of drop-off to the river below. The pines look tiny, covering the mountainside. They are rolling mountains, immense in size, but not jagged.

Our destination was the bottom of the canyon where the river lay. There were switchbacks of dirt road cut into the mountainside near the end of the voyage. They drop down to the canyon's base. Aspens reached their nimble limbs out, scraping the side of our vehicle. Being that we were in a motor home, the scratches rang loudly.

My eagerness always started ramping up at the last stretch, coming down a small hillside bordered by mountain flowers and tall wild grass. In my forward line of vision, the river flowed. The river of the thousands of holes, and I knew almost every one.

When we reached our destination, we tore out of the motor home, the ambience settling us. The sun shone. Walls of trees steadily lined our vision. Birds skittered, singing, at ease in their homes. The warmth of the day was comforting, but seeing the change of colors in the trees reinforced that nights would be sharply cold.

Pitch darkness soon huddled around us. Traces of breath misted the air. The fire, magnificent, spread its warmth as the heat mounted. My eyes adjusted to the night. Further than that, they adjusted to the firelight. "Firelight eyes" are when you can still see beyond camp, but the faces around the fire are held vividly in sight. That is what I saw. My firelight eyes peered at the faces I loved so much, flickers of orange and yellow flowing on their contours, jawlines, and head shapes. I held each person close to my heart, smiles waning through hardships but laughs grabbing hold and carrying us all into a world of our own.

Pine trees stood out darkly, faint whispers of flickering firelight bringing them to life. The smell of sweet smoke sweltered in the night sky while the campfire popped and crackled. We dodged the smoke as whiffs of wind blew it into our eyes. The chill of the night tickled our backs as our fronts roasted.

We crafted marshmallow sticks from moist limbs and angled them over the embers. Some marshmallows came out golden roasted after careful, elegant twisting. Others became fire-covered balls of sugar, mallows burned to be peeled layer by layer. Graham crackers held chocolate to make a sandwich sweeter than should be consumed.

One by one, we started trickling to bed. Fatigue intensifies as night wears on. The fire slowly died, embers glowing and smoke flowing, as chill started to set into the bones. The air grew cold. My sleeping bags felt frozen as I squeezed my warm body in.

This is camping. This is life seen through firelight eyes. Honestly, I was born for this.

In the morning, the inside wall of the tent had a layer of frost on it. The moisture from our breaths through the night made it look like snow. My body was warm, snug, and I did not want to get out of the sleeping bag's cozy folds.

I looked to the others; they were still asleep, heads covered, snoring. I slowly unzipped my sleeping bag. I was still dressed, and the moist smell of old campfire swelled in my nose.

Slipping my boots on, I reached out and unzipped the tent. Murky, cool, humid air escaped as the brisk, chill mountain air snuck in.

I took a step out into the beauty of the frost. It blanketed everything. Grass stood colored by the white. The aspens were losing their yellow leaves one by one. The fire pit lay waiting to be brought back to life. The sun was still hidden behind the mountain, the immensity of the canyon sheltering us from its warmth.

I took a poking stick and jabbed the old coals bit by bit. Puffs of smoke emerged, proving there was still heat beneath the ash. I stirred and jabbed. Then I threw dry grass and tiny chips from limbs in.

Down on my hands and knees, I began to blow, trying to breathe our source of heat back to life. Powdery ash flew and blew. Smoke dispersed, and finally, a flicker of fire took hold.

Everybody started to wake, the look of sleep painted on their faces. The morning's temperature spoke to them. Running their hands up and down their arms, they quickly ambled toward the comfort of the fire. My stomach growled, but I was ready to go fishing. I had my gear set up and lure tied. Eager, I actually made extra noise to wake everyone up.

After Dad made some coffee and we ate a bowl of cold cereal, the beckoning of the water's flow urged us on. The sun slipped above the mountain, pushing the frost with its rising light. Ken was as ready as I was; I caught the glimmer in his eyes.

Gram stepped out of the motor home with her breath whispering by. She sat by the fire, warming up. Love surrounded us all in normalcy, living the dream; our dear little mixed up family.

Wow, that was one of the best times of my life. I will hold onto that memory as a light for my heart.

I know there was so much more to life than what I was living. I didn't want to believe you had to have one or the other though. Bliss or anguish. It seemed easier to have faith in the "in-between." Blah. The waves of uncertainty still ate me alive. I was sick of all of the confusion. That's why on days like this humble camping trip, I soaked in every single moment.

Chapter Twenty-Five

The Dance

Our parents got married at the end of the fall in 1996. It was cold outside that day, not quite winter. Everyone was happy. It was a simple proceeding, calm and inexpensive, held at the LDS church in Spring Glen, Utah.

Honestly, I felt lost. I knew that their weaknesses still held on. I understood the strength well enough. It worried me, but I plastered a smile on my face. It was one of those days when you know you're supposed to express yourself like everyone else. So was I being fake? I am not sure. I had accepted Leesa and my stepsiblings. But vestiges of doubt crawled at the bottom of my pant legs.

The dance was fun with laughter carrying in the air. The room was large with a linoleum floor, and fans covering the ceiling moved the air. Presents were stacked on a table by the book to be signed. Out front, people stood smoking, shivering from the cold. Lights inside were dim. The cake was beautiful yet simple, had three layers, and was homemade.

Then I saw Amber Basso only feet away. She was my Dad's friend Kevin's daughter, my sister Alissa's age, with long blond hair.

My crush was immediate. My first real crush. Instantly, I pulled my lip over my buckteeth. I imagined that the glare of light bounced off my forehead. I was shy, lost in my world, a shell of shame. Still I admired her. Her smile sent shivers down my spine. Her gait was agile as she came toward me, her body slender. The dress she wore was simple. She was beautiful.

Alissa saw the adoration in my eyes and asked her to dance with me. *Oh, hell no!* They both smiled at me. I turned my ugly head away. I wanted to disappear.

I couldn't though. That would look weak. So I stood, focusing on being confident, trying to gain some courage. Next thing I knew, a hand touched my shoulder. I turned my head. Her smell was ambrosia, and she asked me to dance. I nodded, trying not to flash my ugly teeth.

We were close, moving in perfect circles. The sound of the music faded away. We gazed into each other's eyes. I no longer wanted to disappear. I was stuck. No one existed around me. It was her and me. I didn't have to think about the motions. The shape of her face carved from the light.

Just as quickly as it started, it was over. The sound of her voice seemed unreal.

"Thanks for the dance," she said. Then she floated away. Pride lifted me up.

It was a fantastic day, the tying of the knot. Although I felt ambivalent, I was glad to see Dad happy again. His smile was wide and so full of life. After Mom died, I had never expected him to find someone else.

At certain times, I tried hard to accept Leesa. I still held onto my love for Mom and felt that it was somehow a betrayal, that she was up on a cloud crying because I had let her down. Sometimes I just wanted to hate. Shrouds of deep, dark hate. The bitterness of life overtook that last remaining speck of light.

Time felt strange to me. I wished I could make it stop when love pulsed in our lives. Other times, I wished I could fast forward when smacks rang out and abuse echoed. I wished for my own little time machine or remote.

Where I am now in my life, I just want to feel love, for myself and humanity. I'm tired of waiting for the next bad thing, predicting the worst, expecting it.

Intellectual powers are far greater than we can ever understand. We create our reality based off of a belief, a simple thought. We create thoughts based off our desires or fears.

The life we project mirrors what we spin inside. If you fear of being cheated on, then you will be insecure, creating the energy that pushes your loved one into someone else's arms. Yeah, ultimately, it's the cheater's fault, but the energy behind it all can be controlled.

Confidence is loving oneself, knowing that no matter what, you are never alone. You should never search for happiness in someone else. Being a whole person is critical in any positive relationship.

This is where I have failed time and time again. In my seeking for completion, I drained my significant others. My fears created my reality. So here I sit in this drab world of bricks and bland food, alone with my thoughts.

Our parents had left to go to the grocery store, Alissa was watching us, and we had something up our sleeves. All of us kids gathered together to head outside for the day.

Bit by bit, the snowflakes slowed. I gazed off the book cliffs beyond. Blue started to crest the cliffs' border. The clouds were moving, and soon the sweet sun would glisten off the snow.

We stopped in a small valley. Trees surrounded us. We could see our breaths in the air, and we flipped the buckets to sit on.

Ken and I looked at each other. My face felt cold, my nose was runny, but other than that, I was ready to start building.

We started packing the buckets full of snow. Scoop, pack, scoop, pack until one was full. Then we flipped it, tapped the top and sides, and pulled up at the same time to reveal a perfect mold of the container made of snow. We constructed each block carefully and placed them side by side, building walls.

After this was done, two walls across from each other, we crafted each snowball and filled each bucket.

We laughed with each throw, snow balls soaring, heads ducking behind our walls. Feet pumping, diving, and rolling. It was like playing on cold cotton candy with our hearts pounding, sweat pouring, and iciness freezing our faces.

Snow sweat is hard to explain. Wrapped up tight in layers of cloth with cold biting at the nose, movement was hard in the white mounds. We had to fight with each step, breathing hard, and snot running down our faces. Bits of snow falling inside the boots. Body heat melting. Burrowing the snow lower. You have to keep moving, otherwise the cold sets in, and when it does, then comes the bitter end to the fun.

I loved the wintertime. Endless snow, clean and fresh, washed away all of the grime of the year.

We had all been getting along well, leaning on each other, and gaining strength from one another. We sat around the TV, couch cushions swallowing us; our blankets were warm as we grew tired. The parents were downstairs, high on drugs and distant.

Christmas came with lights strewn, twinkling and beaming, songs sung, and the smell of a real Christmas tree filling the living room.

The sunlight beamed through the windows covered in plastic, Dad's attempt to keep the house warm. We pulled out the presents one by one. I felt gratitude, love, and the family as a whole.

I got an electronics kit, something I could make seven things out of like a lie detector or alarm system. It included diodes, an electronic board, and all. On top of that, we got hockey sticks. This was when the Mighty Ducks were big. Ken got a new pocketknife. Wow, it was sharp.

The plastic encasement that seals a product had to be cut off for some of the toys. I swear, they make packages impenetrable. You can't twist and tweak the seal. You can't pull it apart. The only way in is to cut it off.

I asked Ken to help me with his brand-new knife. He started on one side, shoving the tip through, slicing strategically. Then I grew impatient. So impatient that I began yanking, pulling down on my toy.

Blood squirted, hitting the ceiling. Ken stood stunned as his wound appeared horrendous. I was petrified as stone. What had I done? I ran to retrieve Dad while Ken found something to cover the wound up.

This Christmas in Spring Glen, I will never forget! The time when Ken received eight stitches on his hand, and I received a few blue hand marks on my butt.

I remembered being scared to go tell Dad what I had done. I felt literally frozen inside. Yeah, I was scared for Ken as well, but I'd seen the cut, and I knew it would heal. But the transformation in Dad had started to grow worse. Drugs were changing him.

When something struck that nerve, watch out. The change always sent me down the rabbit hole. Honestly, I would say I dissociate. But the memory of his eyes always stayed. When they switched from hazel to black, I would swear he was possessed. The veins in his neck stood out. And when he was *really* mad, there's one on his forehead too. Watch out!

I'm breathing deeply right now as I look back at what I have tried to block. Chipping away the mortar, I see now how scared I really was. I always just wanted to see him as my hero. And he is. But the drugs turned him into something else.

I'm sad. I feel so bad. Dad, I love you so much; you know this. But I have to heal. So I am admitting the facts.

Life. Wow, it's truly a test. I see so much pain in the past. But mixed with it, I see love, honest, deep love. I feel lighter, seeing it and telling it. I can't hold it in any longer. I want to be happy in life, to grow, to be independent, to be successful, and to have a family. I want to have children of my own, to walk the riverbank with my son on my shoulders. I want to sit down by the stream and watch, smiling, as he casts. That is what life should be. Bliss. Joy. Heaven on Earth!

Not sitting in an eight-by-ten-foot cell with a metal toilet right behind me, sounds of other inmates pounding in my head, and the same old smells, filling and blotching everything out there.

I close my eyes. Tears border my lids. Through praying and thinking, I know there is so much more than this. I will choose love every day as I look into the mirror and my own brown eyes and see my head as unique.

I know I'm worthy. I'm building my confidence, not ego. It's a simple understanding that happiness is not defined by possessions or job titles. Happiness is who you are, the choices you make, the spectrum of light you let in. Valuing life, breathing, and your heart beating. Not putting poisons inside to disrupt the flow. I don't have to run anymore. I get to be me and build a life, an amazing legacy.

Chapter Twenty-Six

A Friend's Death

Winter started to slip away. The air outside was still cold, the trees were dead, but spring was coming. I could feel it for sure.

We were outside playing with a ball. PJ had grown up and was running, chasing the ball fast. His paws were bigger, his head was fat, and he moved in an unorthodox way. He was part of the family, and we loved him tons.

I had seen the car coming before I threw, but the ball went flying into the road. PJ raced toward it.

It was an accident. Creepy wheels crunched on the gravel. Mean chunk of steel crushed him. His bones snapped. A bellow burst out. The whole car carried him a few feet. He came scooting out on his front paws, dragging his hind legs behind him.

He kept yelping as the pain ate at him and pushed himself closer to me. My heart fell from my chest, gripping inside. I ran to his aid and fell to my knees, winding my arms around him. Blood smeared my pant legs. He was shaking, moaning, pleading for the release of pain.

The lady driver stopped her car. She watched me holding him as I panicked. She said she was sorry. I'm sure that she was, but I scowled at her, anger boiling beneath the surface. I didn't say anything to her and just sat there, holding my dying friend. I was so scared I was going to lose him, my best friend.

She took off, not knowing what to do. Brit and Bear went inside in tears. We were all in shock

Dad came out, and we carried PJ into the garage. We bundled up some blankets, made it soft, and set him on it. I just wanted to heal him, to mend him, and take away all of the pain.

Tears ran down my cheeks. The whimpers and whining he made were killing me, sounds of anguish tearing at my life. He made the same tone over and over, one of deep, complete suffering.

I didn't want realization to creep in. I wanted to think, to believe that he would stay with us. I didn't know what to do. I sat there lost, taking it all in and thinking that this was what it's like to see death's hands. Menacing and creepy. My dog's soul was about to leave.

Slowly, the cries faded. My dog's breathing calmed, and he relaxed. The only thing that remained was some shaking. A chill set into him. Death's chill. Energy ebbed as his life dwindled. His eyes kept looking at me. I knew he was there until I saw them haze over.

I felt the power of the other side, the hands of God, the source's pulse. Energy swarmed, spinning, making it cold. I felt the pulling on his soul, the comfort wrapping him, the light taking him.

When his pain started slipping, I felt it. His eyes kept staring. I swear they spoke to me. He said that he was okay. I knew it. I trusted.

Then beat, slow beat, slow beat. The rhythm came to a stop. The cadence of death. This cycle was over. I knew it. The glazing eye reflection was gone.

This was the first time I'd seen someone close to me die. It was a terrible, sad, complicated day for us all. PJ had been part of the family. I felt torn apart. We all were. Kneeling in that cold garage on that early spring day, I learned an amazing lesson in friendship, in emotion, and heavenly cycles.

From that day forward, I knew that there was more. There is energy in all life forms. A soul. A divine force derived from the source and grown with personality and emotion.

I thought of PJ tromping around in his spirited way. I imagined him leaning to one side, tongue flopping, and eagerly chasing me. I remembered the way he rolled to be tickled and jumped his front paws on you to be held. How he looked into your eyes, beaming love, beaming light.

Although I learned a great lesson about death on that day, I still made a subconscious vow to not get so close to anything again.

Throughout my life, I've opened up at times. But just barely, and then fear has slammed the door shut. Fear has always controlled my life. I see that now. I understand. We all have lessons in fear, in loss, in deceit. Those all hurt tremendously. We build shells and push people further away. Relationships are fragile, love is misunderstood, trust is nonexistent, and people learn to stay away. It's a guard. A subconscious one.

Shifting Back

Wellington, Utah, was like a magnet. We were always pulled back to the murky confines of sagebrush, cattails, and swamps; steady smells I had grown to know and will never forget.

Spring Glen had run its course. In our restlessness, we surrendered once again and cast off to a new residence. With this move, I hoped we would leave addiction behind. Perhaps that was why we moved. Hope. Desire for better things.

It never works out for us though. Intents can be pure, but until addiction is confronted, it will always remain an infinite weight, black, hollow, and scorching.

We moved into our cousins' old house, a stone's throw from our previous apartments—the blue ones where we'd first lived.

Our new home was a three-bedroom, one-bath with an unfinished basement. The grass was completely dead, and the sun scorched all moisture into the air. We had a carport instead of a garage and a large backyard, barren and in dire need of some life. The best thing about our house was the fact that we lived right by a forest of elms and Russian olives. It was a country boy's dream with activities galore.

The first thing we did was tear into the backyard. Dad crunched away on the hard ground with a huge tiller. The power of the motor, blades, and dirt looked as if it would tear his arms off. He held on, his strength beckoning him forward. He took one small section at a time, tilting back the handles to lift the blades, then setting them into the soil. It was quite the process. I remember taking my turn, and the vibrations nearly ripped my head off.

The next step was to roll and rake the ground flat. We all helped with this part. The smell of the manure Dad tilled into the soil reminded me of our foster-home stay.

I did that a lot, getting sidetracked by sights, smells, and sounds. They took me back to good times and horrible times. Sometimes I would have to shake my head to snap out of a memory I was locked into: Mom's drooping smile. Mom's tilted head, drooling, or her eyes peering and orange and nearly lifeless.

Anyway, we strewed grass seed evenly on the soil, watered it, and then came Dad's trick. He spread hay. He said that it kept the ground from drying, which must have been true, because next thing I knew, new grass was growing. Green perked up from the soil. It all looked so fresh and beautiful, much better than the dry, cracking earth we had before.

I turned twelve years old. I have distinct memories of this time in Wellington although they are sporadic. They span for roughly two years.

Ripples stretch, blotting out innocence like a storm, completely uncontrollable. I stopped looking forward to socially-perceived normality. All that was normal to me was the inconsistency. Such it is for all families caught in addiction. Purpose is unknown. They are lost, falling through the air with no wings, waiting for impact with the ground to bring peace.

What did I hope for from life? Catching a fish. Dad next to me, smiling widely. Barbecues and family togetherness.

Of course, beyond my scars, the demons brought forth bouts of pain, aiming to add to the torment. All it ever did was make it more extreme.

Dad got a new truck, an old 4×4 Chevy, brown and tan. It was an off-road machine, just waiting to be taken for fishing.

I was playing out front as Dad pulled up. He had two motorcycles at the back, and I nearly flew over to the bed of the truck. I'd had no idea that Dad was going to surprise us like that.

We unloaded them under the carport. They were in parts, so I took a few minutes studying them in pieces. The bigger bike was white. Obviously, it would be Ken's. The orange one was mine. It was shorter and built differently. Dad said it was an Enduro.

This would be a great project to take my mind away, I thought. I always enjoyed something new. My thoughts raced. I pictured myself using Dad's tools, screwing here or holding this bolt for him to set.

By this time, Ken came outside to soak it all in as well. These were our new toys, a new experience. I imagined cruising down the dirt road on my motorbike, the piston flying as the spark ignited fuel. The best part was being on two wheels. I would feel the air soaring past, leaving a dust of cloud behind.

We organized all of the parts, cleaned things, and studied them. Dad's understanding of mechanics sank in.

The bikes were missing some piston rings and a few bearings. Specialty parts that, unfortunately, had to be ordered. So we all had to wait until Dad got them ordered in. He said it would probably take a couple of long, impatient weeks.

I understood what it was to cherish the simple things in life: clothing on our backs, food in the fridge, a roof over our heads. Or neat stuff that I cherished like motorbikes, my electronics set, videogames, or Lego.

We were never into social trends. The latest and greatest didn't exist. Our new was new to us, regardless of the actual age. This understanding, the need to cherish everything we had, was ingrained into me. Throughout my life, I have seen things as a necessity.

I understand that ego is directly attached to possessions. It always astounded me to think that to be "special," you had to have the social flare, the best name-brand clothes. Three-hundred-dollar jeans. Ninety-dollar shirts. Image was built upon status like the newest, fastest cell phone. "You are what you own" is a frail image. Crazy.

There are children starving on the streets, dumpster diving or freezing to death, grateful for a bite to eat. Crying because they wander alone. Sick and dirty, in need of a bath. Life for them is one of hunger, pain, sickness, and loneliness.

I have learned to take nothing for granted—a warm bed, a simple hug, love, warm food, and a fridge to keep it in. With each bite you take, be grateful.

The road in front of our home was old asphalt, dry and cracking. Pieces of it fell apart everywhere. About one hundred yards farther down, it turned to gravel, leading under elms to bike jumps, trails, and fields. It was close to the same area where I parked while smoking, and it was a time of great adventures, hiking, and trail riding.

This was the first time I met my neighbors across the street, three brothers with red hair and littered with freckles. Their names were James, Jeff, and John. They were a rowdy bunch raised on farmland. They were tough. They had come into the world with leather hands, ready to throw hay and complete hours of daunting work on the farm.

They used to beat each other up. It was shocking, bordering on sickening. Yeah, my brothers and I went our rounds, but the neighbors made us look as if our fights were merely play. They slammed and cracked their fists hard to each other's heads, faces, and bodies, all the while cursing at the top of their lungs. Their parents didn't intervene and just let them settle their differences. Sometimes I wonder how they turned out or if they are even alive.

The oldest brother was rarely around. He used drugs. He used to wear Jamaican hats, and his long red dreadlocked hair draped out the sides.

I hung out with the middle brother, James. He was my age, and we went to school together. He was not a good person for me to hang out with. I learned and saw things with him that changed me in negative ways for the rest of my life.

I started to take larger steps in the wrong direction by acting out in school. I wanted attention even if it was the wrong kind. I became the class clown, breaking rules, and acting like a fool. In retrospect, I see the shift I made. I finally had a friend, someone I could hang out with. He was tough, and he saw me the same way. We fed off each other.

I can see now that I was lonely, looking for anything to latch on to, any sort of change.

The shift was terrible. I am grateful that I recognized now how long ago it started. The multiple roles I played, lost and faceless. It is deep-seated.

I always have to recognize the importance of being authentic, being open, and honest. I have ran from my past for so long, one addiction after another, seeking escape and comfort. But it's empty. The more I have ran, the more lost I have become.

My criminal lifestyle has been extensive. It started on that day when I was five, stealing those candy cigarettes. It progressed through different levels of crime, mostly revolving around theft.

Now I understand how everything we absorb through childhood molds us. I am not justifying my mistakes. I have made many. I'm an adult, and I made my choices. I'm speaking of the blinders that I see through, the way life is obscured when I peek out, and how the images are tainted. Once the poisons hit me, I went whipping through life, inflated, lost, mindless, and searching for anything to satisfy my latest cravings.

Another point. Friends really matter. I know it is difficult to point your children in the right direction, but being involved in the correct manner actually will help them. Do not control their moves. That pushes them away and leads to dishonesty. They will wear a mask for you and start the road of manipulation.

It's about getting on their level. Can they talk to you about anything? Explain to them what true friendship is, what pain is, and about loss and addiction and how it all feeds into the same realm. Everything they see builds into their beliefs about who they are. Being involved all of the time, with love and understanding, is the key.

We went to the hills of Wellington on the dirt roads. Dust flew in my face as I zoomed after Ken. The motors roared on the dirt bikes, the sun pounded on my back, and I was thankful for the goggles I wore. I handled the gears swiftly: clutch, shift, clutch, shift. Next thing I knew, we were in fifth gear, and the trees blurred past me in streaks of green.

Ken was ahead. I grew closer, throttle open, gravel pattering my helmet. I kept pushing, forcing my little orange bike harder.

I just couldn't keep up. Ken found another gear and quickly lost me. I let off the gas, and the bike slowed. Clutch, downshift, clutch, downshift until I stopped. I pulled over, put the kickstand down, and pulled my sweaty helmet off.

I sat on the side of the dirt road. The grass was soft under me as sweat trickled down my back. We had been riding all day. I was beat and happy that I'd finally learned how to downshift. It had been a few months since we'd gotten the bikes going, and it was difficult enough moving up the gears. The clutch popped time and time again, killing the motor, and frustration breathed through me. I had figured it out, though, how to float smoothly. I felt like a professional as I lay back on the grass, hands behind my head, and rested gracefully.

The air was warm and calm, and it gently caressed away the sweat. I closed my eyes. I remember lying there, drifting in peace. The calm of the world around me expressed itself. The pulse of nature's heart surrounded me. Birds chirped, flying over their land. Trees rubbed leaves together, speaking softly, "Life is perfect." The echo of the pistons' rattle vibrated in wave as Kenny's dirt-bike noise slipped away.

I remember the expression on Dad's face as we put the bikes' elaborate mess together. My desire to ride climbed so that my patience barely held.

Oh, Dad's smile! His voice echoed when something wasn't right, and cuss words floated as his frustration peaked. It was like this throughout my life with Dad. I was his mechanic's helper, handing him tools and making sure the flashlight's angle was just right. Sometimes I started to think of something else, and the beam would slowly angle the wrong way. One word from him brought it right back.

The brim of his hat always seemed to get in the way. He would take it off, showing the top of his bald skull, and usually find something to bang it on.

I felt so important when Dad let me do something on my own. My prudence during the task made Dad laugh. My cautious hands shook so much the socket wrench struggled to find its mark. Eventually, my fingers started to work right. Unsteadiness coasted into confidence as projects slowly fumbled together.

My interest with all types of hands-on projects multiplied. Dad's goading and fix-it-all abilities blundered into me. Keenly watching his crafty ways, I noticed that he could see the end result when he first accepted a challenge. I observed an ability in him that I yearned for.

Even though addiction coursed through our lives, our parents got my brothers and me into sports. The sounds of the bat ringing and catching a ground ball are still part of me. So are memories of wearing my blue-and-white uniform with knee-high socks and the tight bottoms of the pant legs riding all the way up. I wore my shirt tucked in. It felt rough and crispy, almost like wearing a piece of shag carpet. My tiny ankles jutted out of my cleats, and my feet dug deep in the sand.

I remember how the white sand was raked meticulously, the corrugated ripples perfect and almost endless. Fields of forest green, cut purposefully, surrounded the field, and the smells of the fresh manicure fit into my memory.

I love baseball. I always have since my first swing.

Our innocence swelled as the team rose together as one. The cool morning air stirred, brisk enough to wake me up, and helped to pump my slow blood. The ticking of sprinklers in another field warned us of moisture raining, and we narrowly missed the onslaught of artificial rain.

I remember the laughter, the smells of leather and glove oil, the tightness of the new mitt as I fought to break it in. I would stick it under my mattress, enfolding a ball, and wrapped with a rubber band.

The white ball, soft leather, red stitching leached onto your fingers as you reached your arm back and took aim. It was an artwork, pleasurable like a play. The part was written for the love of the game: catch at chest and repeat.

At home plate, I stood with knees slightly bent, staring ahead. The glance of the sun was barely blocked by the helmet's brim. Sometimes I waited with baseball bat in hands, elbows held so the angle of the bat leaned expertly behind my head. The pitcher wound up, timing the ball to fly my way. I shifted my weight on my back leg, hips steady to turn the body eloquently. I sliced the air, ball hit the bat, and perfect toughness pulsed through my body. I took off, feet soaring, and quickly approached the first base.

I wish that I had stayed on the path of sports. What is it to wish? It means regret, desiring something I don't have. Yeah, I may have gone to college, gotten married, and had children. But if I had stayed in sports, the experiences I have had would not have taken place.

Paths are just that, paths. I may be judged for my decisions. But understanding that yesterday is behind me keeps me in the now. The future is a moment waiting to happen, and the energy for tomorrow is daunting.

Chapter Twenty-Eight

Phantoms

The hands of time flew. Volatile days burned into weeks. An inferno raged in me, the change a result of my devious choices. I felt like the actor of a part yet to be written, performing on a whim, on impulses to feed the shadows inside.

I started to drift a little from the family chain, the hardness of our steel. My self-hate kept me swirling under the radar.

When I started to be the mask-wearing boy, people liked me. I had friends, followers, and I was my own leader, driven by the pleasure of my ego. But it was hollow, temporary. I soared above the radar in a plane with no fuel. Of course, the plane had to come down. And when it did, I had to fill the tank back up to fly again. It was unauthentic.

Of course, I still absolutely loved my family. We were inseparable. But the hate inside me caused shifts in my patterns. My anger toward my younger brothers rose. The brotherly torment became a vicious cycle. I broke their stuff just to see their anger, ripping Barbie dolls' heads off, or stomping on GI Joes.

It was weird, my bullying. I was appalled by bullies. I still wouldn't allow it at school. But at home? It was a different story. The psychology behind it still confuses me. Perhaps it was just my way to release some of the pressure that had been building inside.

The incessant chatter and arguments of the world around us obstructed my view of the situation. Dad and Leesa drifted further apart as they continued to taint their consciences with dope.

They didn't have arguments of general disagreement, of voices that barely rose as they found middle ground. Their arguments had a certain shakiness to them, desperation behind the forced words. The energy fanned out, pushing away the rest of the love. It became a kind of heaviness that exerted its power by keeping us kids in our rooms.

Methamphetamine holds in it the souls of hell. Twisted, pale streaks of dawn are scoured by the bonds of the darkest night. When negativity is allowed inside our lives, despair swims freely, singing songs contrived of notes spawned in the pits of darkness.

James, the neighbor kid, and I were hanging out a lot more. Our worlds collided, meshing our messed up minds together. Ideas flowed, and we planned something to fill our time. I was dimly conscious of possible consequences. Frankly, they no longer mattered.

I remembered clearly walking to the convenience store with Kenny and James one cool day. Dirt blew about as we took the shortcut. The smell of stale water circulated in Wellington's air. Weeds towered tall, swaying, all life in them completely gone. It was late summer and dry. Clouds, fluffy and round, moved slowly in the ocean of blue they sailed in. Step by step, our malicious intent beat through us.

I gave them the rundown, rehearsing the plan Dan and I had used before at Guido's. This time, however, we wanted real cigarettes. You see, we were cowboys, and a cowboy wasn't complete without a cigarette in his mouth.

We weren't the cliché cowboys you see on TV. We were merely country boys. Fields of hay surrounded us, dirt fed from the wind, and fun came from playing on the hills.

Texting didn't exist then. Sitting around the house, soft hands striking keys on a phone with a friend on the couch next to you was unheard of. Siri? Ha, ha. Not happening. We figured things out on our own, trial and error. We had dirt under our fingernails; we laid in the mud, shooting BB guns under the glare of the sun.

The store stood there, waiting to be stolen from. Cars pulled in and out, gas pumps churned, and money rang in the registers. Gas was about $1.10 per gallon. Cigarettes? Hmm, maybe $3.00.

It's crazy to me to think it's only been nineteen years. Technology has grown into a savage beast with information on anything only seconds away.

We walked into the air-conditioned environment. One worker stood behind the counter. She watched us and smiled. I checked out the candy aisle nonchalantly with easygoing energy. I'd left my nervousness outside. I simply put my mind somewhere else. My friend sauntered toward the sodas, cold behind the refrigerator doors.

This time, the plan commenced without as much guilt. He dropped his knife, and I stuffed my waistline with the smokes. The thrill of the theft ate me alive. As the lady moved back from behind the sodas, she looked right into my eyes. I smiled and told her to have a good day.

I had stepped over a boundary in which guilt remained quiet in my chest. I found thievery enthralling.

Obviously, we left and started to puff away. I still didn't inhale; I was scared from last time. Ken and I shared some as well. Secretly, we strolled off to "our" forest to enjoy privacy from the world.

I remember actually feeling important when I started stealing. Someone special. It blows me away to think that my patterns had already taken shape.

I do laps like a rat in a cage, constant circles in the day room. Sliding jail doors click in and pop. My thoughts of the past are always running. This was the choice I made. It is what it is, a restricting pattern to learn from.

I'm looking back in my life, writing my story, and dealing with my memories between lines. I'm grateful. I'm working on myself, sorting out layer upon layer of pain. I feel the love of God pulsing through me, forgiveness diminishing my self-hate.

I am making a willful transformation from the muck of the gray. Brilliance comes from understanding the shackles it created. My shackles are bonds of the strongest steel, which pierce the flesh and rip me down under. I was swallowed by my own hands, my own crazy patterns. This is my creation.

Knees on her chest, Dad held Leesa on the bed, hitting her. I stood staring, feeling lifeless. *Dad! Please stop*, I thought. My courage fled.

I'm a coward. My heart pumped, useless. *Why am I here? Can't I stop it?* Shaking, weak, I thought, *What is the point?* I tried. Oh, I tried. Standing there usually worked, kept Dad tamer. Now, though, I seemed to be invisible. Their addiction had pushed me out.

The door to the bedroom stood open. Everything felt as if it was rumbling, caught in a snare, metal barbs gouging deep, causing the worst pain.

I fought deep, searched, mustering all I could. I lifted my heavy hand. I had to be heard. Closing my eyes, I screamed at the top of my lungs. The light came flying out, the sound of my voice stronger than the dark.

My fist found its mark. Sheetrock crumbled by the door.

Thank you, God, for the strength! The fighting ceased.

That is not the way my father is now. He has been clean for nearly ten years. His calm, loving energy today doesn't fit into the times of the past.

Once again, I feel guilt for sharing our experiences. Dad was a shell, his soul buried. Keep that in mind if you, too, hold the poisons, when something other than yourself controls you. Whether it be drugs, booze, gambling, or porn, the power is immense. You lie, cheat, and steal to keep the poisons coming. Life is fragile enough without the mindlessness.

Find something greater to hold on to.

Human potential is astonishing. We truly can do anything we put our minds to, good or bad. Feel grateful for a child's laugh and the energy behind a baby's first word. Or sitting in a rocking chair, wrinkled hands entwined, staring off into the horizon.

Life is like a flower, beautiful, elegant. It needs water. It needs sunshine and soil. It needs balance in temperature and light cycles. When we take away from the necessities, the natural balance, the flower fades away, diminishes, and turns into a lifeless stem.

Chapter Twenty-Nine

River's Torrent

Kenny and James strolled down the gravel road, rocks crunching under our feet, sun beating us, sweat starting, and the essence of sage covered the area. We just wanted to get out of the house to have some fun.

Ken and James walked ahead of me, their young voices mimicking the adults. Profanity flowed freely; we were all faking being grown-ups. I had a piece of dry weed in the edge of my mouth. I thought I was the coolest thing ever.

I was now taller than Ken. His father's genes were strong. His dark brown hair was getting thicker, and crystal blue eyes gleamed like the summer sky. Still, though, our mother's sweet blend smoothed through us, a mixture seen if you looked hard although most people said they couldn't see that we were brothers. Our closeness, our simple knowledge of each other, and our mannerisms generally changed their minds.

Bear and I, however, were a sight to see. We were strikingly similar although he was quite a bit smaller than me. As I said earlier, his nose was broad, but that's about it. The square, angular face I possessed had developed differently from his.

My personality was morphing in all directions. With each trial, a shadow grew, and to hide each shadow, I wore a mask.

The river was deep and winding along the tall banks. Shrubs and small trees lined the water. We approached the large embankment almost like a beach. Dirt and rocks rested under our feet, the ground sloppy and stinky in areas where the water stood still.

I snatched a rock to skip on the water. It was perfect, flat and wide to slap off the surface. The air was still and warm. I threw my arm back in a sidearm, floating the rock out of my hand. *Smack, smack, smack,* the ripples flowed. Ken and the neighborhood kid joined in. It became a contest to see who could ricochet to the other edge.

We stripped off our clothes, thinking skinny-dipping would be a great idea. Standing out there, the bugs and the sun combined with our tarnished smiles.

Taking a deep breath, I prompted myself forward toward the depths of the water. As if it were alive, it pulled on me. Into the air I went, knees to my chest, in a cannonball.

The swift current was splashing. Wow, it was cold! My heart stopped beating in my chest. The undercurrent caught me, whipping and pulling me deep under. The powerful river churned. I stuck my hands out, afraid, because I didn't know where it was going to release me. Kicking brought no escape. The river eagerly gripped me, frisked me, as if it sat there laughing, looking directly into my eyes.

Wham! Just like that, the ride was over. My mobility returned as the river's current let me go. I took heavy, grateful breaths and looked to see where I was. The sun reflected off the water, and I saw that I had gone around the bend. I kicked a few times and pulled myself up to the grass.

The crazy part about that day was that we all continued jumping into the same spot to enjoy the rough water. We pushed ourselves into an area that could have killed us. It didn't matter though. It was fun.

I think this was the beginning of my ultimate risk-taking. I can't remember a day before then that I actually put my life on the line. But after that, "risk" became my middle name.

As an adult, I drove too fast, with no seat belt, and took turns like a madman. I climbed out of the passenger window in my friend's Firebird and held to the top while he flew as fast as he could. I pushed life to the brink of death. It made me feel alert when the rush poured through me. I kept hoping that maybe, just maybe, each stunt would be the end.

Then I started throwing drugs into the mix. *Zing.* Wow. I always drank way too many. I had to drink more than everyone else. That led to kicks to the ribs, arm wrestles, and burning each other.

Pills came next. Round, oval, long, all shapes and sizes. Then came shots of fifty units then one hundred units, so I was "up" for days on end.

With my vision scoured and smeared, all the days meshed into one. I walked around lost, hoping and praying for death. I found myself nodding, slipping, sinking into the couch I sat on. Heroine squeezed and pulled hard on my soul. All I could think was, *God! Take me! Please, I beg you!*

Every time I found love, I crushed it. I was getting too close to normalcy. I wanted to escape into blackness. But, no. My soul swam in the inferno.

Chapter Thirty

Off-road Adventure

Dad threw the chains at the back of the truck. We were bundled up, and the slowly-falling snow was not going to stop us. Dad, Bear, Ken, and I felt determined, bold, set on finding the best real tree ever.

The truck's exhaust spread out in a murky haze due to the temperature. I felt ecstatic, wrapped up tight, and ready to waddle through snow drifts.

Britany and Ethan went to their dad's house for the holidays, so we took the time to head out on our own, the three of us boys with Dad, enjoying life. The pack held strong.

Dad laid the chains on the ground and then drove onto them. Ken gave him the signal to stop. Dad hopped out and hooked them up.

Bear sat between Dad and me. Ken had called "shotgun," cradling the passenger door. The music polished our thoughts, turned low, and settling into our hearts.

Sloshy roads, snowy ruts, and chains gripping. In the 4x4, it was easygoing. This felt so good. We sat shoulder to shoulder, the windshield wipers slowly keeping the fat flakes off the window.

The expanse seemed to be heaven's land, drift after drift, banks of the whitest snow. Trees dropped heaps of weight as the flakes made their limbs heavy. It seemed to be a radiant, holy painting living around our devout troupe of simple men. We honored the hour of life in which flurries of elements whisked by.

Dad was a tower of a country man, a cowboy with a hat and a moustache. He wore jeans with thermals underneath and hunting boots around his big feet. Axe in hand, he stood ready to start the voyage.

Me and my brothers wore snow pants. Standing big, we acted as if the cold was harmless. We were charmed by his simple sturdiness. Backs straight, we pushed with our feet, breaths twisting in the chill, and hearts beating hard from the effort.

We scanned live trees ahead, blanketed with snow, but green as can be. We eyed jubilant needles, full and complete. The trees seemed to urge us, ready to be mounted in our living room. I could imagine gaily wrapped presents in colorful paper placed under the canopy.

Dad shook a blue spruce. Clouds of white fell, providing a better perspective. It emerged, waiting to be taken.

Dad held the axe like Paul Bunyon. He had cleared some snow. Now, on his knees, he chopped. At the base, chips flew, scattering with each swing of the axe. When he was almost through the trunk, he yelled "Timber!" and took it the rest of the way down.

Dragging it back to the truck was excruciating. We fought through endless banks of snow, cold sweat under our snow pants while flakes continued to fall.

I always looked forward to it. I could count on wintertime bringing forth the joy of Dad's 4x4 truck barreling through the extremes, his stereo playing, cigarette smoke filtering in the air. This folded into us a fondness for the mountains, beauty and solitude at every angle, and scraped away everything simmering through us.

These days aligned us in gratitude, arranged us somewhere between the spoils of hell and the pureness of heaven. Sheathed by angels' arms, such days guided us through addiction's madness.

I loved seeing Dad eating up the rough terrain, hands on the wheel and focused. When we left town and entered the sheer magnificence, tranquility literally pumped through our veins. Moments filled with undertones of disjointedness ceased to thrive.

Traditions are so important. They connect people. Family members live for the excitement of being around each other, for simple joys like sitting around the table for dinner, eating a home-cooked meal.

Think about the direction society is heading. Shut the TV off. Put down the remote. Maintain eye contact. We can evolve into the caring, humble society we once were.

In eighth grade, I was such a class clown. Looking back, seeing the things I did for attention, is startling. As an adult, when I'm sober, I have the same sense of humor.

When I came out of my hell, I switched completely from who I used to be, timid, indecisive, and shy. The problem was the person I became, false, lost behind masks, and vacillating with each situation I ran into. This grew tiresome. It weighed on me, and soon I was in a maze of indefinites, wondering which direction I was heading. I had no goal in mind except to be accepted, loved, and wanted.

My girlfriend, Sabrina, sat across from me, our desks face-to-face. She had sleek long brown hair, shiny and beautiful in its radiance. Her pale, white skin was almost translucent and soft as silk. Her green eyes bordered on aquamarine. She was so amazing, perfect. Her angelic form cut sharp like a handful of diamonds.

Our feet slowly inched forward. Our eyes embraced for what felt like eternity. In my nervousness, I recoiled from an act of confidence. Our toes drew closer, my heart thumping. Then they touched and entwined in affectionate innocence. Footsie. It makes me smile to embark on that memory.

The static grew worse. Dad and Leesa continued to argue, pushing closer to divorce. All of us kids sensed what was coming. I know I did. I had been preparing myself for it for quite a while because of the experiences we'd had as a family. The smiles, the laughs, the togetherness despite the strife sustained what we had.

Just being kids would've been nice. Being on guard pushed us into years of emotional noise that forced us to grow up. We learned wisdom from comforting each other through nights of listening to the fights like being tied up with water dripping on your forehead. Either you lose your mind or you survive.

Our parents couldn't do it anymore. Itches just couldn't be scratched. Battling with their aimlessness scattered their love. So, inevitably, they separated. They needed air to breathe, and I understood this. Yeah, I was sad, they were family, but part of me had always lain unattached.

I remember the day. Leesa's new green car parked out front; everything already moved. The tears and sadness hung like ashes in the wind. My eyes were blotched by them. I tried to see, but it was hard. I gave Leesa a hug, held on, and told her that I loved her. I embraced Brittany and Ethan, and our bodies shook. Rivers flowed on the shoulders of our shirts.

This was the end of our temporary chain. The link had snapped. We all blew our separate ways.

Chapter Thirty-One

Back Home

Dad was bouncing around to friends' houses after the split. Kenny, Bear, and I moved back to Grandma's. Her blissful blue house awaited our arrival. We walked into her protection, bound by her touch. Sorrow converged with an ocean of love. The walls around us held certain comfort, the smells of flourishing warmth.

I relaxed, surrounded by the old yellow wallpaper and cobwebs high on the ceilings, the knickknacks, handcrafted doilies, and the Chinese closet that held a treasure trove of dishware. Lamps on old end tables cast a dim, bronze light. There was the familiar linoleum peeling in the kitchen, her gas stove, huge cast-iron pans, and oven mitts hanging on the wall.

I don't think Grandma ever used an electric stove in her life. She hated them. Her food was cooked in cast-iron pans that damn well had never seen soap and water.

I miss so much the food she crafted. Simple and hearty it stuck to your ribs. She didn't own an apron. Expertise came from experience: a pinch of this, a smidgen of that. She rarely needed a recipe.

We rallied around her, an obelisk of inner strength and wisdom. Cinders of our burning slowly extinguished. We started building a new frame, composed on a foundation that was and molding into a cast to last. Gram influenced us in humble ways with her backbone of steel.

Dad fell deeper into his addiction. Meth applied even more pressure on him. It soaked its grasp throughout, pulling on his soul, pushing him further out of our lives.

Adjustments. Well, they came quickly although I often thought about the other half of our family. In my heart, I knew the separation was needed.

All three of us boys shared the small bedroom. Kenny got the single bed. Bear and I shared an old foldout metal-spring bed that Gram pulled out of her closet after clearing out the stuff that had filled it up.

I remembered Grandma coming in our room in the morning to wake us up. Her hand smoothed the blankets lying over us. I felt protected. The coziness moved through me like music, a spirited voice in a combination of peace and divine. She created a tranquil environment. Her white 'fro at dawn made me happy as she turned on the old Big Bird alarm clock.

The broken clock emanated a programmed message. "Wake up! It's me, Big Bird, and it's time to get up! Open your little eyes now. Don't roll over and go back to sleep. One foot out of bed, and now the other. Okay, have a nice day, and don't forget to wind the clock." I will always remember the sound of that clock, her big fingers flipping it on, and the smell of breakfast already thick in the air.

Dad popped into Grandma's house every once in a while. He was struggling; I could see it etched on his face.

Gram's car keys sat on the coffee table. I picked them up proudly. She wanted me to start the car, and I was astonished to be given the task. Opening the front door, I was swept by the morning temperature. The grass lay frozen with dew, and the car windows were glazed with frost. I opened the car door and sat in the seat. Keys in hand, I started it, and I felt important as could be.

Oh, the drive! Grandma cracked me up. When she got upset from drivers cutting her off or getting too close, she put her heavy hand to the horn. When she got irritated, her huge fingers flipped the bird. I can only imagine what others thought seeing an old grandma behind the wheel, horn blaring, her gesture telling them what she thought, her old Dutch blood pumping hard.

We walked to school while living with Grandma. It was a long, strenuous hike. All the way down our street, and block after block after that, up a gradual hill that eventually landed us at school.

West Ridge Middle School was great. I tried hard to pay attention but to no avail. My desire for learning grew less than my desire for approval by others. Teachers grew tired of trying to get me to focus. I became the student at the front of the class with my name constantly on the board. This was unfortunate because I was smart. I wanted to learn, but I didn't want to look like a nerd.

I stood up for myself, toughened by bullying, and sometimes by people who just didn't like who I was. Changing that was nearly impossible, so we settled it in undesirable ways such as meeting off school premises to fight it out.

Thomas was taller than me by at least six inches, definitely more broad, and one grade above me. I'm not going to lie; I was scared. He rubbed old wounds, saying things that made me feel small again. Instead of snapping and getting suspended, rumors of an upcoming fight spread. Oh, great! Now it was going to be a performance.

I went through the school field of green fresh-cut grass, and my friends were in tow. My nervousness was palpable. I focused on the task ahead, a violent mission. I pumped myself up for the fight. Heading for the break in the fence, I mustered my courage. Concentrated.

Taking all the courage that I could. Determined, breathing deep, I pushed forward.

As I approached the fence, I narrowed my eyes fiercely and looked beyond. A group of people stood there, bunched up, ready for the show. My opponent was eager; I could see it in him. He shifted on his feet, dexterous. He had ambition written all over him. What had I gotten myself into? His agility was evident. He gave me a demure smile as I approached.

Everyone was ready. We stood head-to-head, alert. People slowly started to fade back as I slipped into tunnel vision. I stared into his eyes. He was ready for this.

My hands came up, balled into fists, a stance I thought was correct. Confidence reigned in him. I struck, straight left. He blocked it. *Whap,* just like that. He kicked! *What?* He kicked twice before I knew what had hit me. My head rang, I felt wobbly, and I barely stayed on my feet.

I tried to swing again, but my limbs were heavy like spaghetti noodles weighed down with lead. The catcalls around me echoed. It took everything to put in more effort. I staggered and fell to my knees. I felt embarrassed, defeated. He had won.

It was too simple: kicks behind both ears. Amazing. Little did I know, he was a kickboxer. I had been ambushed by his expertise.

Humbly, he stopped and helped me up. It was over, just like that. What everyone had anticipated ended in seconds. The crowd fanned out. My head pounded, but my opponent and I talked for a minute. This was an experience I will always remember. We swiftly became friends and reconciled our differences. I was astonished by his abilities.

At least I had stood up for myself. My distorted belief system was fed by more lies. The way that I made people laugh and advocated for the so-called "nobodys" is just the way I was, and I wouldn't change for anyone. My pride held intact. I didn't see my defeat as a hindrance in any way.

Chapter Thirty-Two

A Simple Gesture

Grandma sat in her recliner, snoozing lightly, with the remote on the end table. I lay on the couch. Bear had a blanket on the floor, and Kenny sat in a chair adjacent to me. I was so comfortable in my life with her and the force she carried. Her vivaciousness wound around me, and yet there was firmness as stable as the ground beneath her. She had a durability made of wisdom, love, and empathy.

She stirred in her chair, her feet hurting. Her diabetes caused suffering, but she tried to hide her affliction. We knew though, my brothers and me.

Next to the remote sat a cup with spare change. It was her way of paying us for a foot massage. I was always happy to massage her large callused feet. In no way did I ever see them as gross.

The swelling in them was prominent, going into her calves. I started at her calves and worked my way down into her heels and toes. She would make these exaggerated noises and facial expressions, tilting her head back. Oh my, the serenity and peace of this, I will always remember.

On the last day of school, I was overflowed with excitement, thinking of days of waking up to nothing but summer fun. No more waking at 6:30 a.m. or going to bed by 10:00 p.m.

I had a backpack full of shaving cream, and I wandered the halls. Kids scattered, their voices energetic, from one place to the next to get their yearbooks signed. The beat of summer sauntered through the school's air, and joy emanated. Yearbooks are childhood pressed into memories with quotes, signatures, and expressions signed for times to last forever.

I remember brown bricks, lockers clicking shut, and skipping classes for fun. The simple laughter permanently rang off the walls. We shuffled, ready to hit the doors. Sunshine beamed down from a cloudless sky, and birds chirped beautifully. We ran down the hill through a perfect slight breeze. School was over, the door shut for another summer. Smiles told stories through faces covered with streams of shaving cream.

The grass was soft and endless in the park. Tall trees of deepest green leaned with limbs full of leaves. We ran, loving being one with the summer's day. Shoes off, we floated in tranquility. Afraid of nothing, our young hearts soaked in the sun. We breathed hard, smeared white with shaving cream that stung our eyes.

We thought those friendships would last forever, cherished. But in a blink, our eyes opened, and years had passed us.

Ace Ventura: Pet Detective was my favorite show ever. All of the million faces Jim Carrey makes. His confidence in the most unorthodox times. The way he walked, bobbing his head left and right, his hair shaped strangely so it stood tall with a wave.

I watched that show hundreds of times and copied Ace's ways. I made them part of me, added my own little twists, and made people laugh at my own expense.

This was about the same time I got braces on my buckteeth. I thank God for this. Medicaid doesn't cover cosmetics, but a kindhearted orthodontist put a set on me. They looked like a truck's bumper covering my teeth.

So there I was, marching through school, through life, mimicking my favorite actor, bobbing my head, acting confident, and wearing my mask. Unexposed. I loved all of his movies, and I think that parts of his roles are ingrained in me to this day.

Grandma saw my love for Jim Carrey. She gave me a magazine, inside of which was a contest to enter. You wrote to a specific address, and though I don't remember all the details, I know you could win Jim Carrey's actual button up shirt from his movie. So I wrote to the address, saying he was my favorite actor and that I loved his movies, and I gave the letter to Grandma to mail.

Lo and behold, a few weeks later, I received a response from Jim Carrey himself! He said he was sorry that I didn't win, but he was glad that I was a fan. He said to do well in school and set my goals high.

When I read it, I feigned excitement. Grandma was so sweet, but I knew from word one that she had written it herself. She tried to hide the fact that it was her writing, but I knew it was unmistakably hers.

I have a huge smile on my face and tears of joy lie in my eyes as I think back to that time, sitting on the couch, letter in hand, knowing her intent.

She knew that I yearned for Dad. She saw it written on my face, in my nightmares when she had to wake me up, when I crawled into bed with her drenched in sweat, or nights spent sitting there on the couch, blinds up, waiting for Dad's headlights to angle into the window.

I would know it was him as he rolled to a stop. Night was when Dad came around. Here was where he crawled. From time to time, he would pop in to shower and see us kids. I would be so happy I'd fly into his arms, ready for his embrace.

Dad got a job at a mechanic shop located on Main Street in Price, Utah. This street is one of old buildings, undersized, grimy apartments, and small businesses.

A few cars drift down the road. Stop signs and stoplights were sparse. Teens still cruised Main Street at night on the weekends. They park off the side as well, enjoying loud music and alcohol, a gathering of sorts before they'd head off to the real party.

There are three movie theaters in Price, all on Main St., and one of them was a dollar theater. This was the theater my brothers and I enjoyed with its torn, rickety seats and the smell of musty popcorn.

Dad's shop was in a white garage building. It had an awning out front where customers could park while they came in to set up appointments. Dad did all of the work underneath the vehicle with floor jacks and body dollies. I loved coming to work with him.

The garage door always shut with a bang. The summer's air felt like a field in heaven, infinite in its comfort, pleasurable and distinguished in a way words simply can't describe.

I mounted the pinnacle of gratitude in evenings spent with my father, in the smells of oil, grime, and rubber. Dirt crawled into my memory. I remembered tools scattered, ratchets clicking, and air tools zipping.

His hands were huge but covered with grease; they fit into tight places that seemed nearly impossible. A bolt here, a nut there, torn to pieces out of one pile. With concentration, the puzzle goes back together, step after step, with a swift agility you can't measure. He was a self-taught master of trial and error.

"It's common sense," he used to say. He could see the workings of things, the dynamics. Patterns jumped out at him. Blueprints flowed in front of his vision. He had no use for books, he just saw the end point. By surveying and inspecting the job, he created the solution.

I used to watch in awe as I handed him this socket or that wrench. I was proud of my simple task. I was dirty like Dad.

It was the summer that shines in my memory. The moments I spent with Dad I held on to diligently. Each second was purposeful and passionately absorbed. My anxieties waned. The heaviness of my mind deflated because racing thoughts advanced to emptiness.

Chapter Thirty-Three

The Distance Between

Dad, the brothers, and I were all inside the new trailer. It was disgusting, a filth created from sloth. A film of neglected dirt mixed with a layer of some sort of oils coated the walls. Years of compounded swamp-cooler air, open doors, and shoes had been added to animals, food, and ignorance.

This was going to be our new home, a single-wide trailer Dad had found for us. It stood on top of a range of hills where other trailers were sparsely spaced. Weeds and dead grass covered the area.

We started renovations in the kitchen with the upper cabinets, shelves, and walls. The wood was rotting, so we attempted to cover the shelves with contact paper. We worked our way down through drawers, counters, and lower cabinets.

Grandma helped us. She was sweaty. We all were. The swamp-cooler needed work. Little germs gripped as we pushed through the mass.

I was in the living room with Jeremy, steadfastly absorbed by our imaginations. Heat soaked in, and we were agitated. I heard Dad muttering under his breath, cleaning the bathroom.

Grandma was in the kitchen, bleach permeating the air. That was her preferred cleaner. The strength of her mix was immense. The rag she cleaned with wouldn't last long. Dissolved by chemicals, it lay in tatters.

I hold on to this memory vehemently, a day in which I quarreled with one shadow and lost. We both sat, plainly scared. The texture of the experience was alloyed in hell.

It started as a game, one I thought would be fun, but Jeremy had complete fear coursing through him. I struck him directly on the left side of his face. The strike rang off the wall. Instantly, my pang of regret overcame me.

Like a storm, panic rose in me. I knew that the punishment would be severe. I had never thought I could smack that hard.

A smacking game? What the hell? What kind of idea was that? My mind had created a game I knew I would win, in which I got the first move and knew he wouldn't slap back if I hit him hard enough.

I'd swung for the fences like a racket hitting a tennis ball. *Whap!* My poor brother took the smack from my hand hard. His brown eyes reflected surprise, which misted into tears.

Time stopped. Betrayed by a mindless action, I was bolted down as Dad came flying into the living room. Jeremy's tears fell, and blood streamed. The cut was deep, obscene.

My action changed everything. I was faithless in who I was and what I had become. How could I? My intent had been to hurt my brother! Which way was I leaning? I know I had a conscience, but where was the emotion?

The expression in Jeremy's eyes told of hurt conflicted by love. He wanted to hate me, but he chose love. Seeing him on that day showed me he still loved me, and I found it revolting. I didn't deserve his love. He should have hated me.

So what did I do? I ambushed any remaining inner beauty. My character was blighted by fear. My worst enemy was myself.

There was no consequence except the look my father gave me, an Arctic gaze. He was confused by the situation. I was frozen inside. Was I crazy? That was the question I asked myself, and it beat like a drum.

After the slapping incident, Dad decided we weren't going to live at the roach hotel. When he asked why I smacked Jeremy, my answer was, "The devil took over me." That is honestly what it felt like. So we continued to stay with Grandma during a search.

I started to fall farther away from everybody. I stood on one side of a canyon, humanity on the other.

Life became plagued by arguments. They occurred almost daily. I took out most of my anger on the ones closest to me.

Grandma sadly took it. She withheld, always remaining objective with her understanding of where my expressions of torment came from.

There is still an island of the unspoken between Jeremy and me. In his presence, I see the imbalance, a bit of denial mixed with a desire for resolution. We are close, but when I have spoken to him on the phone from jail, I hear a lack of care for the burden I have placed on myself. He thinks I place these walls around myself out of mere weakness. The best example is the slap. I had to protect him from me. Protect everyone for that matter.

I stayed behind my own wall, looking over. Everyone I loved was down on the ground, but to get there would have required me to jump.

My fate has been in limbo all of my life, the wall infinite. Now I have a rope tied, and I am climbing down.

When I reach the bottom, I will smash the wall and connect to everyone, a life of love, understanding, and forgiveness, in which I will see through my fear. Remember that judgments are born of fear.

Chapter Thirty-Four

Death's Grip

Dad backed up into the spot in Carbonville, a nearly impossible angle. He had bought us a new home, a single-wide trailer in need of some work.

History had repeated itself; we had moved literally down the street from our first home in Carbonville, the yellow trailer home. Once Dad found the proper angle, he unhooked it from the semitruck. We couldn't get power or gas hooked up until some code was met. In the meantime, Dad hooked up sewer and water.

I began to hear some chatter and strange rumors that caused my mind to shift and go into utter chaos. The rumors were that our dad had been cooking methamphetamine. That was such a scary thought for me to try and process. Images of my father being blown to pieces polluted my dreams. I saw him in nightmares, lying there, arms crossed in a normal casket formation, my hero stuck in that case. Relentless screams shredded away hope, grinding my skin like a cheese grater.

We stayed a few weeks back and forth between Dad's house and then Grandma's house. At Dad's house, we had to use an orange extension cord that we stretched from the neighbor's to our place, powering a lamp or two, our TV, and, of course, the PlayStation.

At 3:00 a.m. and 4:00 a.m., methamphetamines slipped further into reality. New people came over with pick sores torn. The holes they scratched into themselves mimicked chicken pox. I saw frenzies as they tore holes in themselves. Skin meant nothing to them. They left craters like the moon lashed into their flesh. There was a man that was introduced to me one night as Scotty. He had terrible sores on his face, some were still bleeding slightly, and he continued to pick at them. This man stuck in my head because he can, every other day, consistently dressed in the same ragged clothes. He wore a gray hoodie that looked three sizes too big for him with black sweats, and he always wore his slippers. I am not sure if he was a neighbor or lived close by; I just know that he was a consistent visitor, but I never saw him around at normal hours of the day.

It was hard to get sleep with all the disruption during the night. I would often peek out and watch the activity of the visitors as well as my father's behavior with the strangers.

We eventually became used to it as just the daily routine, and it didn't disturb us as frequently anymore. It was not until Jeremy screamed from the bathroom with a piece of glass from a meth pipe stuck in his foot that reality set in even further. We both had known what the glass was from because we had both seen these pipes used by both Mom and Dad throughout our lives thus far. I yanked the piece from Jeremy's foot and had him hold a towel over it with pressure until it stopped bleeding. This image and memory will forever stick with me.

I loved being with Dad regardless. But the void inside me was immense. I started trying to predict fate, to see the future so that I could protect myself. I was not going to lay torpid. With one step closer to adulthood, I felt it was time to be at the mercy of nothing.

Deep down, in emotional holes, lay possibilities for torment. Re-jection by Dad would always hurt. As hard as I tried to be strong, to have a mask of steel, inside, I took the promenade through meadows of thorns that gouged, causing me to disallow the present and turn my head the other way.

Kevin and Bean came with Dad, the brothers, and I fishing. Their quintessence was sealed into memory, the beauty of a day in which rays of sunshine and the land surrounding them spoke of one million words. Pine trees staged everywhere, towering and the deepest green. Crisply, the river scouted down God's land, elegantly feeling its way through the meadow's hold.

Kevin was a short and stout man with ice blue eyes, blond hair parted down the side, and Bean was a mirror image of his father even more each day as he grew older.

Dad and Kevin walked toward me, smiles huge. Laughs sheltered the shifting dread. They had huge fish strung up, blends of brown and gold, reflecting the prism of joy. When drugs were dormant, they floated on a cloud all of their own as their sons ardently sat by, soaking in the moment.

That beautiful day on the railroad tracks was the last memory I have of Bean and the last vision of inner radiance from Kevin.

On a breathless night, Kevin woke to a living nightmare. Kevin lost his son, his one and only, hijacked by fate, an accident washed by tones of sorrow. His life cracked at waking up to Bean's bed left forlorn. Down on his knees, he wept tears of fire, begging God to release him from this dark world. Bean was only sixteen years old. He died from an overdose of OxyContin, a prescription pain medication that had become such a touch of evil that had stolen countless souls.

Desolation trembled the fabric of Kevin's reality. He didn't get any joy out of life after that. He lived empty in a soggy space of anticipation, waiting to follow his son.

Dad and I tried to pull him out of his despair. We would go to his home to see if he wanted to go fishing, but it was like trying to pry out a rusty nail.

Kevin kept all of his son's possessions. Set up exactly as Bean had left them, hoping one day that he would return home. This desire was a poison. It festered and ate at Kevin and took an unspeakable toll on him each day.

Fifteen years later, he gracefully followed his son. Kevin died of a stroke. I like to think that Kevin passed away in my ideal image of putting down his fishing pole, kissed his loved one's goodbye, took his final steps wearing cutoff shorts, and with a tobacco dip in his mouth. I held on to hope that he would be reunited with his son, Bean.

Like an arrow, time flew by. As life does when we began to come of age, memories swiftly separated from each other. The fissures in the time were less shallow, and detachment submerged me into a faceless world where my regard for people lessened. I justified my actions, arguing with Grandma, and plaguing an already trembling reality with my impulsiveness. I was malleable only to my own will, which was deceiving.

At my friend Chris's house in Price, during a sleepover, when his parents were gone, we snooped around his parents' room, looking at dirty magazines and some handguns. My friend's dad was a police officer, and I found the weaponry fascinating. Not to mention the magazines. This wasn't the first time I had seen nude pictures. My dad had owned these kinds of magazines as well, and I had seen them while curiously searching through his stuff.

While rummaging through the closet in Chris's parents' room, I found some money. I took a subconscious note but had no intention of taking it at the moment.

A few months later, Chris stole my girlfriend. I had an idea. I was blinded by the desire to steal the money. My conscience was baffled by turbulent winds, weakened by the shadows I carried with violent tears in the fabric of the webs I'd created. I trudged into the idea, a whole new level of theft.

I had no concern for who I hurt. This family worked hard and saved hard. Here I came, a torpedo of devastation.

A friend stood outside, keeping watch as I entered Chris's empty house. I took the money quickly. A feeling rose up inside me, a rush of fright tinged with thrill.

Walking home to Grandma's with the $1,800 cash in my pocket, the air around me felt cool. Autumn had arrived. The leaves slowly slipped to the ground, tiny sweeps of the air moving their crispy figures.

Inside me rose a mist of anticipation, conscious of the weight of my action, but my devious desire served as justification. I felt condemned, a sham.

When I arrived home, I quickly stashed the money. The guilt ate at me. I gazed over at Grandma then down at the phone.

How could I do it? How could I live with the disdain created by stealing from them?

I called my friend and told him what I had done. The phone felt so heavy in my hand, shaking as I hung up. Sadness and shock melted on Grandma's face. She looked at me, and I felt the sharpness of her regard. It hurt deeply, letting down her devout soul.

I started to further fade away, a conglomeration of wounds seething, invisible even to myself. Who was I becoming?

Grandma opened the door when the police arrived, and I gave her a hug goodbye. His cuffs covered wrists that would feel those steel edges countless times. I was a child gone awry. I felt the depths of iciness as Grandma's tears froze on me when they fell. Inside I exploded, knowing I had destroyed her.

The cop drove me to detention where a cell awaited my arrival. Strip, bend over, and cough. I endured the humiliation, severe in its nature, searching for things I might sneak in. As the steel door closed behind me, my life as it was stopped. I became this, a man behind these walls.

I did not grasp the ramifications of my choices at the young age of thirteen, the vortex born in theft and pornography, two hollow actions. Wafting in spectrum of darkness is "in-between."

The toxicity of nude images has no intent but complete selfishness. When pornography is created and used, so many negative energies are formed. If you look at pornography, humans become objects, separate from their original form. The brain creates a fantasy of sexual desires. They are all experienced carnally, and that creates miles of emptiness between the brain and the soul.

Sexuality should be two people working together, creating passion, making love. In pornography, there is a human behind the camera, swimming, in need of fulfillment and attached to an emotional condition.

I used pornography for my carnal desires and became an addict. Fantasies are created in the brain for a release, an instant gratification. As with any addiction, it doesn't stay at the same level as when you started. It multiplies. Soon what seemed innocuous, like stealing candy cigarettes, turns to $1,800 from a home. Likewise, masturbating once a day to soft porn becomes three times a day to bondage, all while hiding it from your significant other.

These choices build your web. The sickness is unquenchable, and it is driven by fear. Lust feeds inadequacy, which primarily comes from the lack of control in someone's life.

Theft, strangely, is in the same realm, getting away with something, knowingly and strategically living by a reaction that feels uncontrollable.

Being in the abyss, where desultory impulses sink us to the bottom, makes us feel helpless. There is certainly help. By recognizing the steps that lead up to the action, we can pull ourselves out of the fear. Being aware of oneself is living in the moment, visualizing the path. Had I seen the path I was on as a kid, things might have been different.

But if you ignore the visualization of the outcome, eventually you will create what you feared. You will realize that is what you deserve.

This is what happened to me. It is what I thought I deserved. Voluntarily, I saw the guard tower on that day, meant to be menacing, providing protection to society from people like me.

I should have been scared, but I welcomed the gates. I was twenty-two years old, and it was time the riot inside me lashed out. Attachment was my nightmare. Emotions, those scars left on the inside, ravaged me.

I wanted mazes of concrete, the inevitable. I needed it, felt deserving of it, a provenance of wreckage. With bloody fists, I devoured the swamp of fear that prisons hold. Each moment was like being on the edge of a cliff, one wrong move and it's over.

I remember the last fight I got into in prison. It began over a tattoo that I had prepaid for $8 and he had messed it up and was not to my liking. Next thing I knew, I had my hands around a man's throat, on the ground between the toilet and bed in the cell. Inside, I was scattered, taken over by rage, choking him.

When I came to myself, I saw the expression of fear in his eyes. I could see that he truly believed in that moment that I was going to kill him in my unstoppable rage. I only saw red. It woke up my long-sleeping soul, and I started my journey to the light. I found a balance where I almost took the endless step toward death but holding onto love I found the empathy for his slipping life.

That was five years ago. I thank God for lighting the candle inside me. I went from suicide watch due to the attempt of taking my own life followed by finally feeling some light. Although I remained somewhat darkened for five more years, now I am in the sun. The battle is over, the void is full, and I honor life forevermore.

Well from candy cigarettes to smoking real ones, entering someone's home to steal money, or snapping a lock on a gate at a business to steal motorcycles, the progression is stifling, and that is why I am here.

Now I'm wandering through my mind, sifting through my reasoning and seeking recovery. I am still behind locked doors but grateful for the ability to share my experiences.

When I close my eyes, I see my life like a movie, every choice meandering through valleys of darkness. Syringes of meth shots into my veins, bringing an absence of mind that runs a million miles an hour. Heroin, the drug plunging deep. I nod off with cigarettes dropping on my flesh, scorching. Tangled in knots of confused restlessness. The membrane between life and death grew so thin.

Chapter Thirty-Five

A New Life

After five days of incarceration, lying in a hard bed and alone with my frailty, I saw the judge. The sentence was an immediate release with 250 hours of community service. This is the time that the cell should have come to an end and my new life began.

Leaving the correctional facility that day was a moment to rejoice. The morning light shone down, blue skies, and a steady chill wrapped everything.

Dad stood outside of the car, relief from his grief was in his eyes. Our roles had for once been reversed. Here he was picking up his son after five days in detention. I was walking away feeling free and ready to start living again.

My father's warm arms humbly spoke of love, and we both cracked. The hug was galvanizing. In a grim irony, I realized, "Like father, like son." Time had been a torrent of the unpredictable, of destructive, deceptive circumstances. I wished for yesterday to be the child on Dad's shoulders. But I was lost, a servant to only the darkness that was left inside me. A hailstorm of acid corroded everything I touched.

At home, I felt complete. Grandma was always there, so I put away the masks. At night, I cried, the usual nightmares. A dark figure's fingernails slashed at my back.

Gram's love comforted me. I surrendered to cycles and remained constantly on guard but felt it slowly fading away each day. Before bed, we said our prayers. The tone of light shielded us.

We used to watch the *Waltons*. At the end of the show, they said good night to each other as they turned off the lights. We embraced their tradition, making it our own, as each day came to an anxious end.

When the sun started to sink over the book cliffs, sometimes fear started to trickle through. In a recurring dream, minions with huge hypodermic syringes chased me down.

At Grandma's house, the Christmas tree stood. We'd spent the day setting it up, and it was a vision that kindly persevered. The best time of year, with the joy of the holiday, brought pleasure to our lives.

I sat in the kitchen, absorbing rapture and the adoration of gleaming love. My family was so happy. In a symphony of cheer, the music on the radio overflowed. It was an overture of the divine.

At times throughout my life, I have silenced the volume of my most cherished memories. That is when a baleful dredge consumes my happiness. My disregard for laws has resulted in lost freedom. The balance is like a labyrinth, the imposed restrictions kindled in the severed spoils of self-hate.

We drove around at night with Grandma, inspecting the brilliant Christmas lights. Our family enjoyed the holidays' brush strokes, brushed smooth with swinging lights. It's like a painting etched in the mind. A reminiscence of warmth pardoned by the wake of love. My sleeping shadows were held abroad.

Unforgettable and spellbinding, like a storm of shooting stars, Gram's simple touch softened the heart. I ponder on Grandma's ways.

How she recharged us when friction merged with dread. The walk was much easier with her by my side, hand in hand.

Eventually, the sand in the hourglass comes to a stop. It's hard to keep your head held high or your back straight under God's might.

As I lay in bed, I woke to Gram's whimpers from the bathroom. I got so scared. I stood up on wobbly knees and made my way toward her. I found her lying on the ground, and I helped her up onto the toilet, fighting hard. My skinny arms were weak. I should have known. The swelling in her legs had gotten worse. I had forgotten to notice my grandma's pain in each step.

Inside, I knew this was it. That night shattered our strength in agonizing torment and countless questions. Life's storms blew me around aimless.

The hospital's cold doors took her in. Her shell was broken, torn by stage four liver cancer. A steel stretcher held our grandma. The sky rained silent tears, flooding my heart. That was the last night we were together. The tiny blue house has since been torn down, but one thing remains forever, memories of all of us together, tears shed, and nightmares driven away by her warm arms.

I will never forget each breath we all shared. Gram's hand stitched blankets and knickknacks forever live in the beating of our hearts.

When I last saw her alive, antiseptic stench filled the air. The room was freezing, and we all stood nearby. The monitor beeped, a sound I silenced. All I felt was the moment; all I heard was sniffles. Tears fell.

My tears scorched. I gave her a hug. Her body was swollen, but her eyes looked into mine, and I heard her say in my heart, "Just be happy, accept yourself, and never stop loving."

Her spirit was already leaving. I knew it. But that perfect, loving spirit of hers is infinite with us and in the kingdom above.

I wanted to say some things to her, but I didn't. That lost opportunity has always haunted me. I'm sorry, Grandma! I am so damn sorry! I never meant to be mean to you, to argue with you, to hurt you. I know you forgave me. I feel your arms around me now, so warm, and my heart is so full.

Tears fall, but they are tears of love, not shame. The poison inside me is gone. My scars? They are just that, just scars. They no longer have power over me. Each day is new, a breath in light, a breath of acceptance and gratitude.

Since writing this book, I have lost someone very dear to me due to addiction, my cousin, Danny. He is in my story above and played a large role throughout my life. He was never able to win his battle of addition. Rest in peace, Danny.

This is only the beginning of my story; as I grew older, the struggle of addiction became worse, and I got pulled back into self-destruction. Getting out of detention was the easy part. I am now thirty-one years old, happily married and drug-free. However, it was not an easy road, and I feel lucky that I survived.

I will soon explain how I was finally able to reach my happy ending and the struggles that I continued to face with my addiction.

You can never be "addiction free," but you can live a normal, happy life and take it one day at a time. Never give up.

Chapter Thirty-Six

Author's Note

If you have read this far, I want to thank you.

Telling this story was not easy. For many years, I carried these memories quietly, believing that keeping them buried was the only way to move forward. Writing this book forced me to confront parts of my life that I had spent a long time trying to outrun.

The truth is, healing is not a single moment. It's a process. It happens slowly through honesty, accountability, and the willingness to face the past without letting it control the future.

Since the first version of this story was written, my life has continued to change in ways I once believed were impossible.

One of the greatest blessings in my life today is my wife. She has shown me a kind of love that is steady, patient, and real. She never tried to erase my past or pretend that the scars weren't there. Instead, she stood beside me as I continued to grow and learn how to live beyond them.

Another part of my life that means more to me than I can fully explain is the relationship I now have with my father. Like many families affected by addiction and hardship, our story was complicated and painful for many years. But time, growth, and forgiveness have allowed us to rebuild something that once seemed impossible.

Today, our relationship is strong. I respect him deeply, and I'm grateful for the man he is and the bond we share now. It is proof to me that even relationships that have been through darkness can find their way back to something meaningful.

This book is not only about the pain of the past. It is also about what can happen when people choose to grow, to forgive, and to keep moving forward.

If you see parts of your own story in these pages, I hope you remember this:

Your past may shape you, but it does not have to define you.

Even the most shattered beginnings can lead to something whole.

— **Jessy Spruell**